Nay Chil Ma

Mrs. Ma's Japanese Cooking

Mrs. Ma's Japanese Cooking

By Nancy Chih Ma
Sachiko Ma
Helen Ma Yamawaki

Japan Publications, Inc.

Front Jacket
Variety rice (p. 106)
Back jacket
Pork balls (p. 33)
Marinated cucumbers with shrimp (p. 89)

© 1980 in Japan by Nancy Chih Ma

Photographs by Toshihiro Imamura

Published by
Japan Publications, Inc., Tokyo, Japan

Distributors:
United States: *Kodansha International/USA, Ltd., through Harper
& Row, Publishers, Inc., 10 East 53rd Street, New York, New York
10022.* South America: *Harper & Row, Publishers, Inc., International
Department.* Canada: *Fitzhenry & Whiteside Ltd., 150 Lesmill Road,
Don Mills, Ontario M3B 2T6.* Mexico and Central America: *
HARLA S. A. de C. V., Apartado 30–546, Mexico 4, D. F.* British
Isles: *International Book Distributors Ltd., 66 Wood Lane End,
Hemel Hempstead, Herts HPZ 4RG.* European Continent: *
Boxerbooks, Inc., Limmatstrasse 111,8031 Zurich.* Australia and
New Zealand: *Book Wise (Australia) Pty. Ltd., 104–8 Sussex
Street, Sydney 2000.* The Far East and Japan: *Japan Publications
Trading Co., Ltd., 1–2–1, Sarugaku-cho, Chiyoda-ku, Tokyo 101.*

First printing: September 1980
ISBN 0–87040–463–6
LC 79–1964

Printed in Japan

Japanese cooking is a special but easy way to prepare wholesome, nourishing, attractive meals. Learning how to cook is considered a necessary and graceful art important to all Japanese ladies. This book, which contains many tested recipes, is dedicated to all of those people who wish to master this popular cuisine. It is our hope that it will provide an excellent beginning for you.

Preface

My family is so cosmopolitan that we resemble a small United Nations. There are nine Chinese, four Germans, and four Japanese in the family; and a Japanese, a Philipina, and an Ethiopian take care of my seven grandchildren. One evening, as we were dining on Chinese sweet-and-sour pork, German sauerkraut and sausages, Japanese sukiyaki, and the universal hamburger, my brother walked in and laughingly asked what country he was in.

I believe this is the way it should be. It would be wrong of me to try to limit our diet to Chinese dishes. Nor would I want to, for we all like Japanese foods because of their natural flavor and high nutritional values. For this reason, we serve them often. Moreover, Japanese dishes are frequently artistically beautiful. For example, radishes cut to resemble roses or turnips cut like chrysanthemums are decorative additions to any meal. Sometimes plates are lined with fresh maple or chrysanthemum leaves. A sprig of fragrant pine suggests the New Year, and spring is brought to the table in the form of lightly salted cherry blossoms. In fact, there is a leaf or bloom for table use to symbolize most of the major Japanese holidays and all the seasons of the year.

Freshness is an essential element in the Japanese cuisine. The Japanese climate establishes four distinct seasons, with foods intimately related to each. For instance, in autumn, one of our Japanese friends travels all the way from Tokyo to bring freshly harvested autumnal rice from Niigata because this rice is considered the best in the country. For climatic and other reasons, different parts of the nation produce their own regional specialities. The cold waters off the shores of Hokkaido provide the best salmon. Chinese cabbage from Nagoya is thought excellent. Fish from the Seto Inland Sea is considered a great delicacy, and Wakayama produces fine peas.

Three of the great classics of the Japanese cuisine are sashimi (the freshest possible raw fish or shellfish sliced thin and eaten with various garnishes), sukiyaki, and tempura. At first try, when I was a very young student, I did not like sashimi. Since then, however, it has become one of my favorites for its delicacy and textural variety. Sukiyaki, both an international dish and a national favorite, is more than a century old. The name is said to derive from a practice among poor farmers of the past who cooked meat and vegetables on the blade of a plow (suki). Today special skillets have replaced this original humble vessel, and great ingenuity is employed in preparations. But sukiyaki is not difficult. It is one of the many Japanese meals that are cooked while being eaten and by the eaters themselves in an atmosphere of warm companionship. Tempura, an equally famous dish, is deep-fried shrimp, fish, vegetables, and other ingredients. In the distant past, the Japanese used little oil in cooking; but influences from outside have altered this. Tempura takes the cook's full attention. The ingredients must be carefully prepared, the dipping batter just right, the oil in the frier exactly the correct temperature, and the frying time neither too long nor too short. In addition, tempura must be served at once, for its delicious crispness will not last. Since most other Japanese foods, however, are less demanding in terms of time, they may be prepared in advance and served at room temperature.

I have many years of experience in the field of Chinese cooking and have written many books on the subject. But, as I indicated at the opening of this preface, I and all my family prize the Japanese cuisine and are eager to do what we can to bring it to as wide an audience as possible. This book is one step in that direction. In writing it, I have enjoyed the invaluable cooperation of my daughter-in-law Sachiko Ma, who was a source of information on the traditional aspects of Japanese cooking, and my daughter Helen Ma Yamawaki, who provided ideas for ways to suit Japanese foods to modern living. Throughout the project, our aim has been to adjust Japanese dishes to the ingredients and ways of living of the West. We shall be very happy if our efforts win new international friends for this ancient Japanese style of cooking and eating.

NANCY CHIH MA
January 1980

Contents

Foods for Entertaining

Shabu-shabu

    1 lb (450 g) very thinly sliced, lean
      beef
    2 chopped scallions
    ½ lb (220 g) Chinese cabbage
    1 cake bean curd
    ¼ lb (100 g) *harusame* noodles
    ½ lb (220 g) boiled Japanese noodles
    3 thin slices fresh ginger

DIPPING SAUCE

    4 Tbsp soy sauce
    4 Tbsp lemon or lime juice
    4 Tbsp sesame-seed paste (see note on
      p. 13)
    ½ cup chopped scallion

1)   Mix sauce ingredients.
2)   Arrange meat attractively on a serving dish. Put the softened *harusame*, boiled noodles, and vegetables in a separate dish.
3)   At the table, heat soup stock. Season with salt. Add scallion and ginger. Keep the pot boiling throughout the meal.
4)   Each guest picks up the meat he wants with chopsticks and swishes it in the seasoned, boiling stock until it is done. The cooked ingredients are then dipped into sauce in small bowls provided ahead of time. Overcooking toughens the meat (In North China, where this dish originated, lamb is preferred.)
5)   When all the meat has been eaten, add the vegetables, *harusame*, and noodles to the broth remaining in the pot and cook till done. Serve them together with the broth in soup bowls.

Serves four.

Fig. 1
Shabu-shabu

Chicken Hot Pot (*Mizutaki*)

(see illustration on p. 22)

> 1 lb (450 g) unboned chicken meat (thigh or breast)
>
> water
> 2 scallions
> 14 oz (400 g) Chinese cabbage
> 4 oz (100 g) edible chrysanthemum leaves *(shungiku)*
> 1 cake bean curd *(tofu)*
> 8 *shiitake* mushrooms
> 2 spinach
>
> DIPPING SAUCE
> 1 cup stock
> 4 Tbsp soy sauce
> 2 Tbsp sakè or dry sherry
>
> CONDIMENTS
> chopped scallion
> 1 lemon

1) Cut the unboned chicken into bite-size chunks.
2) Slice the scallions diagonally.
3) Wash *shiitake* mushrooms and discard stems.
4) Wash chrysanthemum leaves; break off and discard roots.
5) Parboil three or four leaves of Chinese cabbage.
6) Parboil spinach.
7) Roll spinach inside Chinese cabbage leaves and cut the rolls into pieces 2 in (5 cm) long.
8) Cut the remaining raw Chinese cabbage into convenient lengths.
9) Cut bean curd into six equal parts.
10) Arrange all of these ingredients attractively on a serving dish.
11) In a deep, heatproof casserole, bring water to a boil. Removing scum as it forms, cook chicken in this water for twenty minutes over a high heat.
12) Provide each guest with a small bowl containing sauce prepared by mixing the sauce ingredients.
13) Add the other ingredients to the boiling pot, a little at a time. Guests eat directly from the pot and dip morsels of meat and vegetables into the sauce, which they season as they like with condiments.

Serves four.

Broiled Chicken Brochettes

(*Yakitori*) (see illustration on p. 18)

> 1 lb (450 g) boned chicken meat
> 2 scallions
> 6 oz (170 g) small, hot, green peppers *(shishito)*
> bamboo skewers
>
> SAUCE
> 2/3 cup soy sauce
> 1/2 cup sugar
> 1/3 cup sakè or dry sherry

1) In a saucepan combine soy sauce, sugar, and sakè. Boil till reduced to about 2/3 of its original volume.
2) Cut chicken meat into bite-size pieces.
3) Cut scallions into pieces 1 in (3 cm) long.
4) Skewer chicken meat, alternating it with scallions and hot green peppers as shown in the illustration on p. 18.
5) Place a wire grill over a high flame and broil the skewered meat and vegetables till nearly done. Dip them in sauce and return briefly to the flame. Repeat two or three times. Serve at once.

Serves four.

Mixed Iron-plate Grill

(*Teppan-yaki*)

> 4 beefsteaks
> 4 shelled, deveined prawns
> 4 mushrooms
> 1 sliced onion
> 1 sliced sweet potato
> 1 clove chopped garlic
> 2 green peppers
> 10 oz (280 g) fresh bean sprouts

Fig. 2   Mixed iron-plate grill, or *Teppan-yaki*

salt, pepper, soy sauce, sakè or dry
sherry

DIPPING SAUCE A
   2 Tbsp sesame paste*
   ½ cup soy sauce

DIPPING SAUCE B
   ½ cup soy sauce
   1 tsp lemon or lime juice
   1 tsp sugar
   1 Tbsp sakè or dry sherry
   4 Tbsp minced scallion

1)   Prepare the two dipping sauces by combining the ingredients in separate bowls.
Halve and seed the peppers; wash and drain
the bean sprouts.
2)   In front of your guests, heat an iron
griddle very hot; brush it with oil.
3)   Season the steaks with salt, pepper, and
garlic. Brown on both sides then cut into
strips. Cook a little longer, then cut into
cubes. Cook to the desired doneness. Guests
eat the meat immediately, dipping the
pieces into the sauce of their choice.
4)   Oil prawns, onion, sweet potato, and
onion. Grill them, seasoning with salt, pepper,
and soy sauce and serving as soon as they
are done. Guests dip these ingredients too
into the sauce of their choice.

Serves four.

* If commercial sesame paste is unavailable,
make your own by toasting sesame seeds in an
ungreased iron pan and grinding them in a blender or with mortar and pestle.

Japanese Hotchpotch (*Oden*)

2 round fried bean-curd patties (*gammodoki*)
2 square *gammodoki*
4 fried fish-paste patties (*satsuma-age*)
2 fish-paste rolls (*chikuwa*)
2 hard-boiled eggs
4 in (10 cm) piece edible kelp
6 cups broth
1 Tbsp sweetened sakè (*mirin*) or sweet sherry
3 Tbsp soy sauce
3 Tbsp sugar
3 Tbsp sakè or dry sherry
1 Tbsp prepared Chinese-style mustard

1) Pour hot water over *gammodoki, satsuma-age, and chikuwa* to remove oil.
2) Halve *gammodoki, satsuma-age*, and hard-boiled eggs.
3) Cut *chikuwa* into diagonal pieces about 1 in (3cm) long.
4) In a large pot or casserole bring water, to which has been added the strip of kelp, to a boil. Discard the kelp.
5) Add all other ingredients, except mustard, and return to the boil. Lower the heat and simmer for from thirty minutes to one hour. Serve the ingredients in deep bowls with generous helpings of the broth and with a garnish of mustard.

Serves four.

Sukiyaki (see illustration on p. 19)

1 lb (450 g) thinly sliced beef
2 cakes lightly toasted bean curd
2 sliced onion
4 oz (100 g) *harusame* noodles or *shirataki*
4 oz (100 g) spinach
4 *shiitake* mushrooms
4 eggs

SAUCE
⅔ cup soy sauce
⅓ cup sakè or dry sherry
⅓ cup sugar
½ cup water or stock

1) Cut each cake of bean curd into six equal pieces.
2) Soften *harusame* in hot water, plunge them into cold water, drain, and cut into convenient lengths.
3) Wash spinach and cut into convenient lengths.
4) Clean the *shiitake* mushrooms and discard the stems.
5) Arrange these ingredients and the beef attractively on a serving dish.
6) In a saucepan combine the sauce ingredients and mix well. Bring the sauce to a boil.
7) In front of your guests, heat a deep iron skillet. Rub it well with beef fat or oil. First cook the beef and the onions. Then add enough of the heated sauce to float these ingredients. The guests may begin eating as soon as the meat is as done as they like it. Each guest breaks a raw egg into a small bowl provided for the purpose, mixes it lightly, and dips the hot meat and vegetables into it before eating.
8) Lower the heat to slightly less than medium and continue cooking meat and other ingredients until all have been used.

Serves four.

Fig. 3 Japanese Hotchpotch, or *Oden*

Fig. 4
Seafood pot

Seafood Pot

> 1 sea bream
> 2 slices cod
> 1 squid
> 4 prawns
> 4 scallops
> 7 oz (200 g) unshelled crab legs
> 4 clams
> lemon wedges
>
> STOCK
>
> 8 cups water
> ⅓ cup sakè or dry sherry
> ¼ cup soy sauce
> ½ Tbsp salt
> 1 tsp sugar

1) Combine the stock ingredients in a large pan and bring to a boil.
2) Scale, clean, and thoroughly wash the bream.
3) Skin the squid. Flatten it and score with a knife in a crisscross pattern. Cut it into fairly large pieces.
4) Peel and devein prawns.
5) Chop the crab legs into large chunks.
6) Soak the clams in salt water to remove sand.
7) Cook all of these ingredients in the prepared stock for from fifteen to twenty minutes.
8) Serve with soy sauce and lemon wedges.

Serves four.

Beef

Braised Beef and Bamboo Shoots

Fig. 1

1 lb (450 g) sliced lean beef
1 lb (450 g) fresh boiled* or canned
   bamboo shoots
2 Tbsp green peas
2 Tbsp oil
1 Tbsp sakè or dry sherry
4 Tbsp soy sauce
1 tsp sugar

1) Leave the beef in slices or cube it.
2) Drain bamboo shoots and cut into convenient pieces.
3) Heat oil in a heavy pan. Stir-fry beef (Fig. 1), and bamboo shoots for a few minutes (Fig. 2). Add seasonings and bring to a boil. Simmer for from five to fifteen minutes, or until the beef is tender.
4) Meanwhile, boil green peas till tender, drain, and reserve.
5) Stir the meat and bamboo shoots together with the green peas and serve at once.

Serves two.

Fig. 2

* To prepare fresh bamboo shoots, follow this procedure.

1. Discard the tip of the shoot and cut vertically in half from top to bottom. ▶

Fig. 3 Braised beef and bamboo shoots

▶ 2. Peel away outer coverings until only the white inner shoot remains.

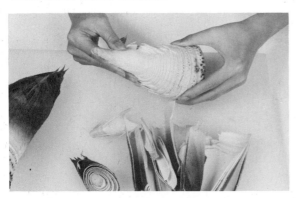

4. Cut in half.

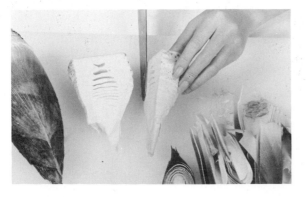

3. Scrape well.

5. Boil for about one hour. Turn off heat and let stand in the water overnight.

Broiled chicken brochettes, or *yakitori* (p. 12)

Sukiyaki (p. 14)

Fig. 4 · Layered cabbage loaf

Fig. 5

Fig. 6

Fig. 7

Fig. 8

Layered Cabbage Loaf

    1 lb (450 g) cabbage
    1 lb (450 g) ground pork, beef, or
        lamb
    2 beaten eggs
    1 Tbsp soy sauce
    2 Tbsp cornstarch
    1 tsp salt
SAUCE
    ½ cup stock
    2 tsp soy sauce
    2 tsp cornstarch mixed with 2 tsp
        water

1) Separate cabbage leaves, wash, and parboil. Drain well.
2) Mix meat with 1 egg, soy sauce, cornstarch, and salt.
3) Line a bowl or mold* with ⅓ of the cabbage leaves. Pour ½ of the remaining beaten egg over them (Fig. 5). Top with ½ of the meat mixture (Fig. 6). Add another layer of cabbage leaves and pour the remaining egg over them (Figs. 7–9). Top with the meat mixture and the remaining leaves (Figs. 10 and 11).
4) Place the bowl in an oriental-style steamer or on a rack in a deep pot with 2 or 3 in (5–8 cm) of boiling water in the bottom (Fig. 12). Cover tightly and steam for fifteen minutes.
5) Combine all sauce ingredients except the cornstarch mixture in a saucepan and bring to a boil. Thicken with the cornstarch mixture.
6) Turn the cabbage loaf out on a serving plate, cut into serving pieces, and coat with the sauce (Figs. 13–17). Serve at once.

Serves four.

* A loaf pan with a lift-out bottom makes a convenient mold.

Fig. 9
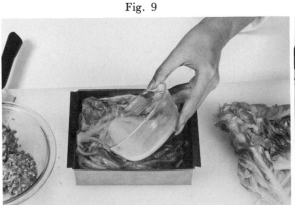

Fig. 10

Fig. 11

Fig. 12

Chicken hot pot, or *mizutaki* (p. 13)

(top to bottom) Beef in sukiyaki sauce (p. 25), Miniburgers in oriental sauce (p. 29), Beef *teriyaki* (p. 25), Beef-and-asparagus rolls (p. 28)

Fig. 13

Fig. 14

Fig. 15

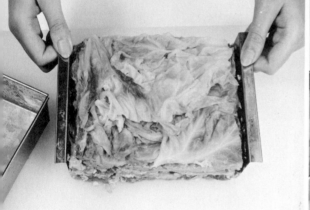

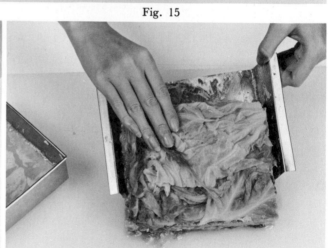

Fig. 16

Fig. 17

Fig. 18 Corned beef and eggs

Corned Beef and Eggs

    3 eggs
    1 small can corned beef
    1 Tbsp soy sauce
    ½ Tbsp stock

1)   Beat eggs. Add soy sauce and stock and mix well.

2)   Remove corned beef from can and flake with a fork. Add to the egg mixture and combine thoroughly.

3)   Heat oil in a frying pan and fry as scrambled eggs.

Serves two.

Beef Teriyaki (see illustration on p. 23)

    1 lb (450 g) boneless beef cut into
       about 12 thin slices
  MARINADE
    2 Tbsp *mirin* (sweetened sakè) or
       sweet sherry
    2 Tbsp soy sauce
    1 tsp grated fresh ginger root
    oil

1)   Combine *mirin*, soy sauce, and ginger. Marinate the meat in this mixture for one hour.

2)   Preheat grill or frying pan. Grill meat to the desired degree of doneness. If you are using a frying pan, add some of the marinade to glaze the meat.

Serves two.

Beef in Sukiyaki Sauce
(see illustration on p. 23)

    1 lb (450 g) thinly sliced beef
    ½ cake bean curd
    1 sliced onion
    3 Tbsp soy sauce
    1 Tbsp sugar
    ½ cup sakè or dry sherry
    oil for frying

1)   Heat skillet; add oil. When oil is hot, sauté onion.

2)   Add beef. When onions have become translucent, add bean curd.

3)   Add seasonings and cook until all liquid has evaporated (Fig. 19). Serve hot.

Serves four.

Fig. 19

(top to bottom) Peppery deep-fried pork (p. 32), Japanese-style pork cutlet (p. 34), Ginger-pork sauté (p. 32), Pork balls (p. 33)

(upper) Chicken-and-vegetable stew (p. 38)
(lower) Chicken steamed in sakè (p. 41)

Beef-and-asparagus Rolls

(see illustration on p. 23)

9 thin slices beef
9 stalks fresh green asparagus
2 Tbsp soy sauce
1½ Tbsp sakè or dry sherry
1 Tbsp cornstarch
1 Tbsp oil

1)   Boil asparagus in salted water till just tender. Cool under running water and drain well.

2)   Wrap beef slices around three stalks of asparagus (Fig. 20), secure with toothpicks, and sprinkle with cornstarch.

3)   Heat 1 Tbsp oil in a skillet (Fig. 21). Fry the rolls on all sides till the meat is brown (Fig. 22). Add soy sauce and sakè (Fig. 23) and continue cooking for two minutes, turning from time to time.

4)   Remove rolls to a serving plate and take out the toothpicks (Fig. 24). Cut the rolls into 1-in (3 cm) slices (Fig. 25). Serve at once.

Serves four.

Fig. 20

Fig. 21

Fig. 22

Fig. 23

Fig. 24

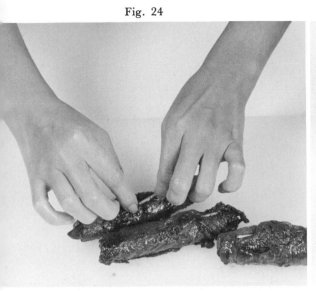

Fig. 25

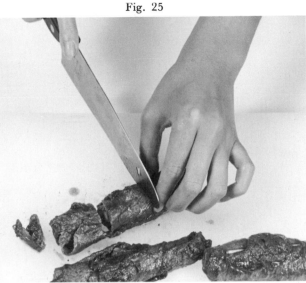

Miniburgers in Oriental Sauce

(see illustration on p. 23)

        1 lb (450 g) ground beef
        1 tsp salt
        1 Tbsp soy sauce
        1 Tbsp sakè or dry sherry
        4 Tbsp chopped scallion
        1 egg
        1 tsp ginger juice
SAUCE
        ½ cup stock
        2 Tbsp sakè or dry sherry
        2 Tbsp sugar
        4 Tbsp soy sauce

Fig. 26

Fig. 27

1) Thoroughly mix ground beef, salt, soy sauce, sakè, scallion, egg, and ginger juice and form the mixture into small patties.
2) Heat oil in a heavy pan and brown the miniburgers on both sides (Fig. 26).
3) Combine the sauce ingredients. Bring to a boil. Pour the sauce over the miniburgers (Fig. 27), and simmer until the liquid has evaporated.

Serves four.

(top to bottom) Deep-fried fish (p. 47), Salt-broiled sea bream (p. 50), Fish braised in soy sauce (p. 44)

(top to bottom)   Clams steamed in sakè (p. 60), Pan-broiled scallops (p. 58), Butter-sautéed oysters (p. 57)

Pork

Peppery Deep-fried Pork

(see illustration on p. 26)

        1 lb (450 g) bite-size pieces of pork
        2 Tbsp soy sauce
        1 Tbsp black pepper
        1 Tbsp cornstarch
        5 cups vegetable oil

1) Marinate the pork in soy sauce and black pepper for fifteen minutes (Fig. 1).
2) Roll the meat in cornstarch and deep fry. Serve hot.

Serves four.

Fig. 1

Fig. 2

Fig. 3

Ginger-pork Sauté (see illustration on p. 26)

        4 pieces, 1 lb (450 g) in all, boneless
            pork loin
        4 Tbsp soy sauce
        2 Tbsp sakè or dry sherry
        1 tsp sugar
        2 tsp grated fresh ginger
        2 Tbsp oil
        1 Tbsp cornstarch

1) Slit the edges of the pieces of pork.
2) Marinate the meat in soy sauce, sakè, sugar, and grated fresh ginger for twelve hours or overnight.
3) Heat oil in a skillet. Coat pork lightly with cornstarch and sauté till brown on both sides (Figs. 2 and 3). Pour in the marinade and simmer till the pork is well glazed. Marinated vegetables are a good accompaniment for this dish. (The pork may be oven roasted.)

Serves four.

Fig. 4 Pork braised
in bean paste

Pork Braised in Bean Paste

> ½ lb (220 g) sliced pork
> 2 Tbsp soybean paste *(miso)*
> 1 cup stock

1) Cut the pork into 1-in (3 cm) cubes.
2) Heat 1 Tbsp oil in a skillet. Fry pork for a few seconds. Add stock and bring to a boil. Reduce heat and simmer for fifteen minutes.
3) Add bean paste and simmer till pork is tender. Serve hot.

Serves two.

Pork Balls (see illustration on p. 26)

> 1 lb (450 g) minced pork
> 3 Tbsp chopped scallion
> 1 beaten egg
> 1 tsp grated fresh ginger
> 1 Tbsp soy sauce
> 4 Tbsp bread crumbs
> ½ tsp salt
> 1 Tbsp sakè or dry sherry
> 2 Tbsp cornstarch
> oil for deep frying

SAUCE

> 1 Tbsp sakè or dry sherry
> 2 Tbsp soy sauce
> 2 Tbsp sugar

1) Combine all ingredients and mix thoroughly. Form into balls about chestnut size.
2) Heat oil. Deep fry the balls until they are golden brown.
3) Combine sauce ingredients in a saucepan. Bring to a boil. Add meatballs and simmer over moderate heat, turning the balls until they are well coated with sauce. Remove from the pan. The balls may be skewered for serving or they may be combined with boiled Chinese cabbage in a casserole (Fig. 5). Sautéed *shiitake* mushrooms or boiled snow peas are a good garnish (See illustration on back jacket).

Serves four.

Fig. 5

Japanese-style Pork Cutlet

(see illustration on p. 26)

>2 boneless pork chops about ¼ lb
> (100 g) each
>salt
>pepper
>2 Tbsp flour for each chop
>½ egg
>5 Tbsp bread orumbs
>1 Tbsp water
>oil for deep frying

GARNISH

>shredded cabbage and carrot
>lemon wedges

SAUCE

>Worcestershire sauce or Japanese
> *tonkatsu* sauce

1)   Pound the pork chops with a mallet or beer bottle.

2)   Slit the edges to prevent curling during frying.

3)   Sprinkle both sides of each chop with salt and pepper.

4)   Beat the egg and dilute with 1 Tbsp water.

5)   Dredge the meat in flour and dip in beaten egg then in bread crumbs, pressing to make sure the coating adheres well (Fig. 6).

6)   Heat oil for frying. Fry the cutlets until they are golden brown.

7)   Serve on a mound of shredded cabbage and carrot garnished with lemon wedges. If you wish, you may further accompany the meat with potato, spinach or tomato. The Japanese customarily dip each piece of meat in a small dish of *tonkatsu* sauce before eating.

Serves two.

Fig. 6

Pork-and-eggplant Fry

>½ lb (220 g) ground pork
>4 small eggplants
>¼ minced onion
>1 Tbsp soy sauce

BATTER

>2 eggs
>1 Tbsp flour
>½ cup bread crumbs

1)   Slice eggplants crosswise into ½ in (1.5 cm) slices (Fig. 8).

2)   Mix ground pork, onion, soy sauce, and 1 egg.

3)   Coat one side of a slice of eggplant with flour (Fig. 9). Put 1 Tbsp of meat mixture on it, spread, and make a sandwich with another slice of eggplant (Fig. 10).

4)   Beat the remaining egg. Dip the eggplant-pork sandwich into flour, then into the egg, and finally into bread crumbs. Continue till all ingredients have been used.

5)   Deep fry these sandwiches as if they were cutlets.

Serves two.

Fig. 7   Pork-and-eggplant fry

Fig. 8

Fig. 9

Fig. 10

Chinese-cabbage Rolls

1 lb (450 g) Chinese cabbage
1 lb (450 g) ground pork (beef or
   lamb may be substituted)
2 beaten eggs
1 Tbsp soy sauce
2 Tbsp cornstarch
1 tsp salt

SAUCE

1 Tbsp soy sauce
1 tsp sugar
1 Tbsp sakè or dry sherry
1 Tbsp cornstarch
1 cup liquid reserved from the
   steaming process

1) Separate cabbage leaves. Wash, parboil, and drain.
2) Mix meat, 1 egg, soy sauce, cornstarch, and salt.
3) Spread a cabbage leaf on a bamboo rolling mat (Fig. 12). Spread the meat mixture on it and roll it firmly (Figs. 13 and 14).
4) Steam in an oriental-style steamer or in a dish on a rack in a deep pot with 2 or 3 in (5–8 cm) of boiling water in the bottom for fifteen minutes.
5) Remove to a serving plate. Cut in sections.
6) Heat sauce ingredients, stirring constantly. When the mixture thickens, pour it on the cabbage rolls. A few boiled snow peas make an attractive garnish.

Serves four.

Fig. 11   Chinese-cabbage rolls

Fig. 12

Fig. 13

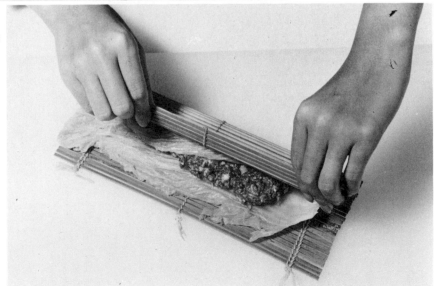

Fig. 14

Chicken

Chicken-and-vegetable Stew

(see illustration on p. 27)

> 1 lb (450 g) chicken meat
> 2 Tbsp oil
> 1 (4 oz or 100 g) lotus root
> 2 small carrots
> 5 dried *shiitake* mushrooms
> 2 stalk broccoli (about 20 pods snow
>   peas may be substituted)
> 2 Tbsp *mirin* (sweetened sakè) or
>   sweet sherry
> 6 Tbsp soy sauce
> 1 Tbsp sugar
> 2 cups chicken stock or water

1)   Cut the chicken into chunks about 1 in (3 cm) long.

2)   Peel lotus root, cut into bite-size wedges, and soak in water.

3)   Peel carrots, cut into chunks the same size as lotus-root pieces.

4)   Soak mushrooms in warm water for fifteen minutes, discard stems, and cut caps in half.

5)   Parboil broccoli, cool in running water, and separate into small florets (if snow peas are being used, string and parboil).

6)   Heat 2 Tbsp oil in a deep pan and briefly stir-fry all vegetables, except the broccoli (Fig. 2). Add stock and bring to a boil. Simmer about five minutes. Add chicken, *mirin*, soy sauce, and sugar. Cover and simmer for from twenty to thirty minutes or until the chicken is done and the vegetables are tender. Before serving, sprinkle with broccoli or snow peas (Fig. 3).

Serves four.

Fig. 1   Ingredients for chicken-and-vegetable stew

Pan-braised Chicken

1 chicken breast
2 Tbsp soy sauce
½ Tbsp sugar
1 Tbsp sakè or dry sherry
1 Tbsp vegetable oil

1) Heat 1 Tbsp oil in a skillet. Sauté the chicken on both sides till brown.
2) Add remaining ingredients and simmer slowly until all liquid has evaporated.

Serves one or two.

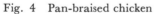

Fig. 4 Pan-braised chicken

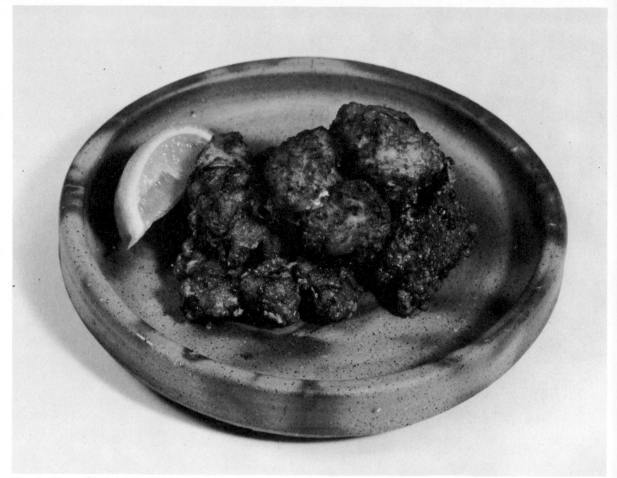

Fig. 5   Deep-fried chicken with seasoned sauce

Fig. 6

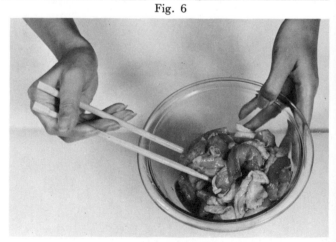

Deep-fried Chicken with Seasoned Sauce

    1 ½ lbs (700 g) chicken meat cut
      frying style
    3 Tbsp cornstarch
    oil for deep frying
MARINADE
    4 Tbsp soy sauce
    1 Tbsp sugar
    2 Tbsp sakè or dry sherry

1)   Mix marinade ingredients. Marinate the chicken in the mixture for fifteen minutes or longer (Fig. 6).

2)   Coat marinated chicken in cornstarch and deep fry till golden brown (Figs. 7 and 8).

Serves four.

Fig. 7

Fig. 8

Fig. 9

Chicken Steamed in Sakè

(see illustration on p. 27)

1 lb (450 g) boned chicken breasts
½ tsp salt
2 Tbsp sakè or dry sherry
lemon
aluminum foil

1) Perforate the chicken skin with a fork or score it with a knife (Fig. 9).
2) Put the chicken on a sheet of aluminum foil (Fig. 10) and sprinkle with sakè and salt. Let stand for ten minutes.
3) Wrap the foil around the chicken and put it in an oriental-style steamer or on a rack in a deep pot with two or three in (5–8 cm) of boiling water in the bottom. Cover and steam over a high flame for twelve minutes. (The chicken may be roasted in the oven for fifteen minutes.)
4) Cut the steamed chicken into pieces and serve hot or cold, with lemon wedges and a mixture of soy sauce and mustard.

Serves four.

Fig. 10

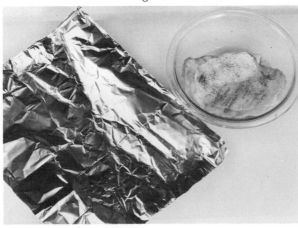

Fig. 11   Chicken and bean sprouts with mustard sauce

Fig. 12

Fig. 13

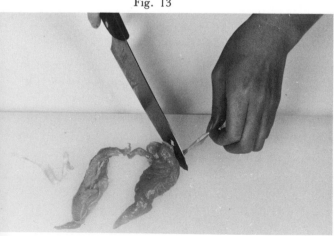

Chicken and Bean Sprouts with Mustard Sauce

6 oz (170 g) skinned and boned chicken breasts
7 oz (200 g) bean sprouts

SAUCE

1 Tbsp mustard
3 Tbsp soy sauce

1)   Remove the stringy roots from the bean sprouts (Fig. 12) and boil in plenty of water for about one minute. Remove and drain in a colander.
2)   Remove the tendons from the chicken breasts (Fig. 13). Boil for about one minute or until the meat turns white. Plunge into cold running water at once. Shred.
3)   Combine bean sprouts, chicken meat and mustard sauce. Serve cold.

Serves two.

Fish

Fig. 1   *Sashimi*, sliced raw fish

Sashimi, Sliced Raw Fish: Sashimi, considered one of the great glories of the Japanese cuisine, consists of any of a large variety of fish or shellfish, sliced with masterful skill and served decoratively with sauces and garnishes. The fish must be of the freshest and must be correctly cut, since appearance is as important as texture and delicate flavor to successful sashimi. Consequently, many Japanese prefer to eat sashimi in restaurants or have the ingredients cut, prepared, and delivered by the neighborhood fish dealer. In the photograph, the ingredients are the ever-popular tuna (*maguro*), sea bream (*tai*), a white-flesh fish called *hamachi*, shrimp, and squid. *Daikon* radish cut to almost unbelievable thinness and fineness is customarily a garnish. Each piece of fish is dipped into soy sauce flavored with oriental horseradish before being eaten.

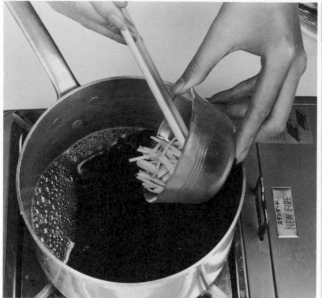

Fig. 2

Fig. 3

Fig. 4

Fish Braised in Soy Sauce

(see illustration on p. 30)

> 12 small mackerel or sole (4 slices
>   if sole is used)
> ⅓ cup soy sauce
> 2 Tbsp sugar
> 1 Tbsp sakè or dry sherry
> ½ cup water
> 2 Tbsp shredded ginger

1)   Clean the fish, wash in salted water, and dry thoroughly.

2)   In a saucepan bring to a boil the soy sauce, sugar, sakè, and water. Add the ginger and the fish (Figs. 2 and 3). Simmer for fifteen minutes (Fig. 4).

3)   During the simmering, tilt the pan from time to time to ensure that the fish is well-coated with the sauce. Cook uncovered till the liquid is reduced by half.

4)   Arrange the fish on a serving dish and coat with 2 Tbsp of the sauce from the pan.

Serves four.

Braised Fish

> 4 slices sole or other white fish
> flour
> 2 scallions
> 2 slices fresh ginger
> 3 Tbsp oil
> 1 Tbsp sakè or dry sherry
> 4 Tbsp soy sauce
> 2 Tbsp sugar
> 1 cup stock

Fig. 5   Braised fish

Fig. 6

Fig. 7

1)   Coat fish slices with flour (Fig. 6).
2)   Heat oil and brown fish lightly on both sides.
3)   Add ginger, scallion, soy sauce, sakè, sugar, and stock. Bring to a boil, cover, and simmer for ten minutes (Fig. 7).

Serves four.

Fig. 8   Foil-broiled fish

Foil-broiled Fish

> 4 slices mackerel (or salmon)
> 3 Tbsp soy sauce
> 2 Tbsp sakè or dry sherry
> 4 *shiitake* mushrooms
> 1 scallion
> 8 thin slices fresh ginger
> salad oil
> lemon
> aluminum foil

1)   Marinate the fish in the soy sauce and sakè for from fifteen to twenty minutes.
2)   Remove and discard the *shiitake*-mushroom stems and cut the caps in half.
3)   Cut the scallion in eight equal pieces.
4)   Coat four pieces of aluminum foil large enough to wrap the fish slices with salad oil (Fig. 9). Put a fish slice on each piece of foil and top with scallion, mushrooms, and ginger slices. Wrap and seal (Figs. 10 and 11).

Fig. 9

5)   Put a wire grill on the burner of a gas range or over hot charcoal and roast the wrapped fish for from ten to fifteen minutes. Or roast for the same amount of time in a medium oven. Serve with lemon wedges.

Serves four.

Fig. 10

Fig. 11

Deep-fried Fish (see illustration on p. 30)

4 sole, mackerel, or flounder
sakè or dry sherry
salt
flour
oil for frying
DIPPING SAUCE (Ponzu)
    2 Tbsp lemon juice
    2 Tbsp stock
    2 Tbsp soy sauce

1) Wash and dry the fish and score at 1-in (3 cm) intervals on both sides to form a diamond pattern (Fig. 12). Sprinkle with sakè and salt. Rub well with flour (Fig. 13).
2) Heat oil (180 degrees C or 350 degrees F). Deep fry the fish until golden brown. Drain on a rack or on paper towels.
3) Serve with small bowls of a dipping sauce made by combining the listed ingredients.

Serves four.

Fig. 12

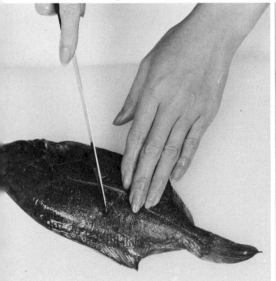

Fig. 13

Fig. 14 Yellowtail teriyaki

Yellowtail Teriyaki

    4 slices yellowtail *(buri)*
    2 Tbsp sugar
    2 Tbsp sakè
    4 Tbsp soy sauce
    3 Tbsp salad oil

1) Heat oil in a skillet and brown the fish slices on both sides.
2) Combine sugar, sakè, and soy sauce. Discard the oil from the pan and add the combined ingredients (Fig. 15). Cook over a medium heat, constantly ensuring that the fish is well coated with sauce, until the liquid has evaporated (Fig. 16).

Serves four.

Fig. 15

Fig. 16

Butter-fried Salmon

    4 slices salmon
    2 Tbsp butter
    ½ tsp salt
    2 Tbsp soy sauce
    pepper

Fig. 17　Butter-fried
　　　　 salmon

Fig. 18

1)　Sprinkle salmon with salt and pepper.
2)　Melt the butter in a frying pan over a
medium heat (Fig. 18). Add the salmon
slices one by one (Figs. 19 and 20). Turning
from time to time, fry for six or seven minutes, or until brown.
3)　Add the soy sauce and turn off the heat.

Serves four.

Note :　A few drops of salad oil added to the
pan will prevent the butter from burning.

Fig. 19

Fig. 20

Fig. 21   Steamed fish with bean curd

Steamed Fish with Bean Curd

    2 cakes bean curd
    4 slices fish (cod or sole)
    4 shrimps
    14-in (35 cm) strip dried kelp
    4 dried *shiitake* mushrooms
    1 tsp salt
    4 Tbsp sakè or dry sherry
    2 tsp chopped scallion
SAUCE *(Ponzu)*
    2 Tbsp lemon juice
    2 Tbsp soy sauce
    2 Tbsp stock or water

1)   Wipe kelp with a wet cloth and make an incision down the middle of the strip.
2)   Cut each bean-curd cake into four equal pieces.
3)   Cut the slices of fish in half.
4)   Shell and devein the shrimp.
5)   Soak the dried mushrooms in warm water till softened. Remove and discard the stems. Make a decorative cross incision in the top of each cap.
6)   Put the kelp in the bottom of a deep casserole or pot. On top of it, arrange the bean curd, fish, shrimp, and mushrooms. Sprinkle the sakè and salt on top of the ingredients and steam in an oriental steamer or cook covered in a medium oven for about twelve minutes.
7)   Combine the sauce ingredients and serve in separate bowls with the steamed fish **and** bean curd. Garnish with chopped scallions.

Serves four.

Salt-broiled Sea Bream

(see illustration on p. 30)

    4 slices sea bream
    salt
    salad oil

1)   Lightly salt both sides of each slice of sea bream about ten or twenty minutes before cooking time.
2)   Lightly oil and thoroughly heat a frying pan and sauté the fish slices about three or four minutes on one side. Turn and cook till done. Salt cooking is the best way to bring out the flavor of seafood and freshwater fish.

Serves four.

Shellfish

Fig. 1   Tempura

Tempura

12 shrimps
3 prawns
6 oz (170 g) white fish fillets
    (sole or smelt)
6 oz (170 g) squid
6 slices lotus root
6 fresh *shiitake* mushrooms
2 green peppers *(shishito)*
1 sweet potato
1 onion
oil for frying

BATTER

1 cup flour
1 egg
¾ cup ice water

DIPPING SAUCE

½ cup soy sauce
½ cup *mirin* (sweetened sakè) or sweet
    sherry
1 cup water
¼ cup shaved, dried bonito *(katsuo-
    bushi*; if unavailable, substitute a fish
    stock for the water)

GARNISH

½ lb (220 g) grated *daikon* radish or
    turnip
2 tsp grated ginger

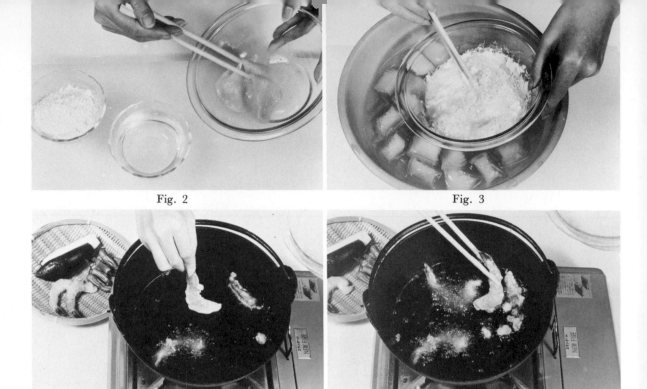

Fig. 2　　　　　　　　　　　　Fig. 3

Fig. 4　　　　　　　　　　　　Fig. 5

1) Peel and devein shrimp and prawns, leaving the tails on. Cut the prawns in fourths lengthwise.

2) Cut the fish fillets into bite-size pieces.

3) Skin the squid and cut into bite-size pieces.

4) Soak the lotus-root slices in water to prevent discoloration.

5) Remove and discard *shiitake*-mushroom stems.

6) Seed the peppers and cut into quarters.

7) Peel the sweet potato and cut into rounds.

8) Slice the onion into rounds.

9) Beat egg and mix well with enough cold water to make 1 cup (Fig. 2). Blend in the flour lightly and quickly (Fig. 3).

10) Heat oil (180 degrees C or 350 degrees F). When the oil is the right temperature, a few drops of batter dropped into it will surface before settling all the way to the bottom and will remain spinning about on top.

11) Combine dipping sauce ingredients in a saucepan. Bring to a boil and drain, then cool.

12) Assemble all the ingredients to be fried on a platter. Dip a few, one at a time, into the batter and lower them gently into the hot oil (Figs. 4 and 5). Fry till crisp and drain. Serve at once with the dipping sauce and the garnishes, added to the sauce as desired.

Note : A few hints about preparing this famous and popular Japanese dish. The batter must be neither too thick nor too thin and must not be overbeaten. Mix with only a few strokes of spoon or chopsticks. It is permissible to leave it slightly lumpy. To ensure crispness, keep the batter cold by setting the container in a bowl of ice water. Do not try to batter all the foods at once and do not fry too many pieces at a time. Dip each piece into the batter separately. Drain the fried foods well and serve immediately since crispness cannot be maintained for more than about three minutes after frying.

Serves six.

Fig. 6   Fried prawns

Fried Prawns

8 prawns
½ tsp salt
pepper
4 Tbsp flour
1 egg
½ cup bread crumbs
oil for frying

GARNISH

4 leaves cabbage shredded
lemon

1)   Peel and devein prawns and make two or three slits on the undersides to prevent curling during frying (Figs. 7 and 8).

Fig. 7

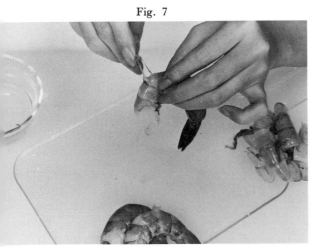

2)   Salt and pepper the prawns. Beat the egg in a separate bowl. Flour the prawns, dip into the egg then into the bread crumbs (Figs. 9–11).

3)   Heat oil for frying (180 degrees C or 350 degrees F). Lightly tap off excess bread crumbs and gently lower the prawns into the hot oil. Turning occasionally, fry till golden brown.

4)   Serve with a mound of shredded cabbage and lemon wedges.

Serves four.

Fig. 8

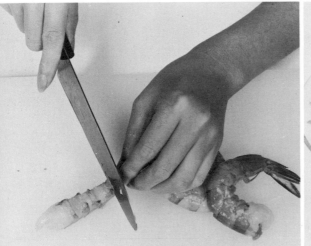

Fig. 9

Fig. 10

Fig. 11

Squid Teriyaki

    1 squid
    4 Tbsp soy sauce
    2 Tbsp sugar
    1 Tbsp sakè or dry sherry

1)   Wash and skin the squid and score it with a knife in a pine-cone pattern. Cut into large bite-size pieces.
2)   Parboil the squid and drain.
3)   In a saucepan combine soy sauce, sugar, and sakè and bring to a boil. Add the squid. Return to a boil. Remove the squid and cook the liquid in the saucepan until it is somewhat reduced in volume. Return the squid and coat it well with the sauce.
4)   Remove the squid and quickly fan it to improve the luster (*teriyaki* means something that has been roasted or broiled to have a shiny appearance).

Serves two.

Note: Do not overcook. Prolonged exposure to heat toughens squid, shrimp, and shellfish.

Fig. 12   Squid teriyaki

Fig. 13 Squid and cauliflower

Squid and Cauliflower

    1 squid
    1 cauliflower
    2 hard-boiled eggs
    1 Tbsp sugar
    4 Tbsp vinegar
    1 tsp mustard
    ½ tsp salt
    1 tsp soy sauce

1) Clean and skin the squid; putting salt on the fingers will make it easier to skin by reducing slipperiness. Wash thoroughly under running water. Cut into rings or slices. Score with a knife. Parboil for five minutes and drain.

2) Separate cauliflower into florets. Parboil and drain. Time can be saved by boiling the egg and the cauliflower together in the same pan at the same time (Fig. 14).

3) Shell and cut the eggs in half.

4) Arrange cauliflower, squid, and eggs on a serving plate.

5) Make a sauce by combining sugar, vinegar, mustard, salt, and soy sauce. Pour the sauce over the other ingredients on the serving platter.

Serves four.

Fig. 14

Fig. 15   Vinegared crab and celery

Fig. 15   Vinegared crab and celery

Vinegared Crab and Celery

> 7 oz (200 g) canned crab meat
> 2 stalks celery
> VINEGAR SAUCE *(Sanbaizu)*
> ⅓ cup vinegar
> 1 Tbsp sugar
> ⅓ tsp soy sauce
> ⅓ tsp salt

1)   Carefully pick over the crab meat to remove all pieces of membrane (Fig. 16).
2)   Scrape the celery and chop.
3)   Combine crab and celery. Combine the sauce ingredients, mix well, and pour over crab and celery. Serve cold.

Serves four.

Fig. 16

Crab Meat and Cucumber Salad

> 2 medium cucumbers
> ½ lb (220 g) Alaskan crab leg meat or
>   canned crab meat
> SAUCE
> 1 lightly beaten egg yolk
> 6 Tbsp vinegar
> ½ tsp salt
> 1½ Tbsp sugar
> 1½ tsp cornstarch
> 1½ Tbsp water

1)   Wash cucumbers. Without peeling, slice thin. Sprinkle with salt and squeeze out as much moisture as possible.
2)   Pick over the crab carefully to remove all membrane. If Alaskan crab legs are being used, cut the meat into 1 in (3 cm) lengths.
3)   Arrange cucumber slices and crab on a serving dish.
4)   In the top of a double boiler combine all sauce ingredients. Stirring constantly with a wire whip or a rotary egg beater, cook over hot water till the sauce thickens. If you do not have a double boiler, in an ordinary saucepan, combine vinegar, salt, and sugar. Heat this mixture. Combine cornstarch and

water. To this add the lightly beaten egg yolk. Stirring constantly, pour this mixture into the heated ingredients and simmer gently till the sauce thickens. Cool the sauce.

5) Pour the sauce over the cucumber and crab meat and serve cold.

Serves four.

Fig. 17 Crab meat and cucumber salad

Butter-sautéed Oysters

(see illustration on p. 31)

> ½ lb (220 g) shucked oysters
> ½ tsp salt
> 1 Tbsp butter
> lemon

1) Clean the oysters by putting them in a colander, sprinkling with salt, and gently shaking under running water. Drain.
2) Melt butter in a frying pan (Fig. 18). Sauté the oysters until they are the desired degree of doneness (Fig. 19).
3) Season to taste (Fig. 20) and serve with lemon wedges.

Serves four.

Fig. 18

Fig. 19

Fig. 20

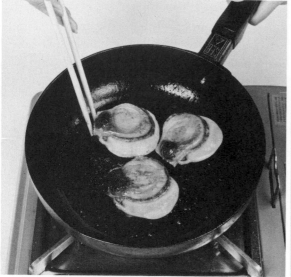

Fig. 21

Fig. 22

Fig. 23

soy sauce and sakè (Fig. 22). Shaking the pan to prevent sticking, continue cooking until the scallops are well-seasoned (Fig. 23).

Serves four.

Clam and Scallions in Bean-paste Sauce

½ lb (220 g) shelled clams
6 scallions

SAUCE

5 Tbsp soybean paste *(miso)*
3 Tbsp vinegar
2 Tbsp sugar
1 tsp mustard

1) Wash clams well.
2) Cut scallions into 2-in (5 cm) lengths. Drop into boiling water for a few minutes (Figs. 25 and 26). Remove and drain.
3) Boil clams for few minutes (Fig. 27). Remove and drain.
4) In a blender, blend the sauce ingredients (Fig. 28).
5) Mix clams and scallions. Pour the sauce over them and mix well (Fig. 29).

Serves four.

Pan-broiled Scallops

(see illustration on p. 31)

8 shelled scallops
2 Tbsp soy sauce
1 Tbsp sakè or dry sherry
2 Tbsp oil

1) Wash scallops.
2) Mix soy sauce and sakè in a bowl.
3) Heat oil in a frying pan and sauté the scallops till they change color (Fig. 21). Add

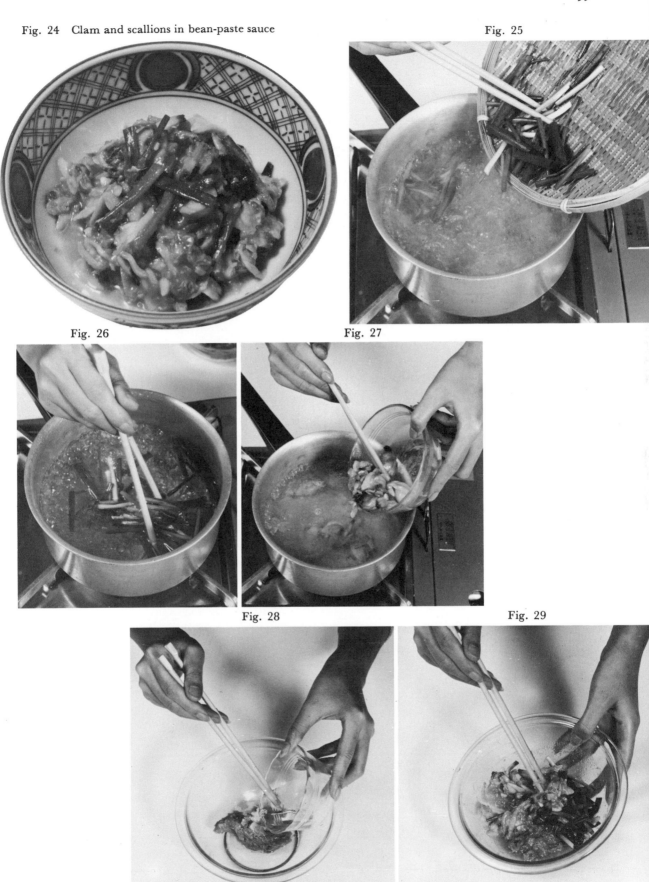

Fig. 24　Clam and scallions in bean-paste sauce

Fig. 25

Fig. 26

Fig. 27

Fig. 28

Fig. 29

Fig. 30

Fig. 31

Clams Steamed in Sakè

(see illustration on p. 31)

1 lb (450 g) short-neck clams in the
shells
1 Tbsp shredded ginger
¼ cup chopped trefoil or parsley
2 Tbsp oil
1 cup sakè or dry sherry
1 tsp salt

Fig. 32

1) To remove sand, soak the clams for two
or three hours in salted water in which you
have put a clean iron nail.

2) In a frying pan heat oil and sauté the
ginger and unshelled clams over a high heat
for two or three minutes (Figs. 30 and 31).

3) Add sakè, cover tightly, and steam for
five minutes (Figs. 32 and 33).

4) When the clams have opened, sprinkle
them with salt and chopped trefoil or parsley
(Fig. 34) and serve at once.

Serves four.

Fig. 33

Fig. 34

Eggs

Fig. 1   Japanese-style timbale

Japanese-style Timbale

(Chawan-mushi)

3 eggs
stock, 4 times as much as the volume
  of the eggs
1 tsp soy sauce
½ tsp salt
½ tsp sakè or dry sherry
4 shrimp
3 dried *shiitake* mushrooms
4 oz (100 g) boned chicken meat
4 string beans

1)   Shell and devein the shrimp.
2)   Soak the mushrooms in warm water till softened. Remove and discard the stems.
3)   Beat the eggs well. Do not allow them to foam. Combine them with four times their volume of stock. Add soy sauce, salt, and sakè. Strain.
4)   Cut the chicken meat into bite-size pieces and sprinkle with soy sauce and sakè.
5)   String the beans, parboil them in salted water, and cut in half.
6)   Arrange shrimp, mushrooms, chicken, and beans in the bottoms of four or six individual custard cups or similar containers

Fig. 2

Fig. 3

Fig. 4

(Fig. 2). (All may be combined in one large casserole, for which steaming time must be proportionately lengthened.) Pour the strained egg mixture into the containers (Fig. 3).

7) Put the cups in a large baking pan and pour boiling water around them till it comes half way up their sides (Fig. 4). Bake in a moderate oven for fifteen minutes or until the custard is set. It is natural for liquid to form on the top of the custard.

Serves four.

Note: Steaming in an oriental steamer is a better way to cook these custards.

Steamed Egg and Chicken Layers

(see illustration on p. 66)

¼ lb (100 g) ground chicken meat
1 egg
4 hard-boiled eggs
4 Tbsp bread crumbs
2½ Tbsp sugar
½ tsp salt
1 Tbsp *mirin* (sweetened sakè) or
   sweet sherry
1 tsp crushed fresh ginger
2 tsp and 2 Tbsp cornstarch
1½ Tbsp soy sauce

1) Mix ground chicken, bread crumbs, soy sauce, *mirin*, ½ Tbsp sugar, ginger, and one egg.

2) Put the mixture in a square pan (Figs. 5 and 6). Steam in an oriental-style steamer for fifteen minutes. Remove from pan and set aside.

3) Separate the whites and yolks of the hard-boiled eggs. Mash the whites and force them through a strainer (Fig. 7). Combine with 1 Tbsp sugar, ¼ tsp salt, and 1 tsp cornstarch. Mash the yolks, force them through a strainer, and combine with 1 Tbsp sugar, ¼ tsp salt, and 1 tsp cornstarch.

4)   Line the same pan in which you steamed the meat with wax paper. Put the egg-whites mixture over the bottom (Fig. 8). Sprinkle cornstarch over it and top with the steamed meat. Sprinkle this too with cornstarch, then add a layer of egg-yolk mixture (Fig. 9). Steam the whole thing for another twelve minutes. Remove from the pan and cut into squares. Serve hot or cold.

Serves four.

Fig. 5

Fig. 6

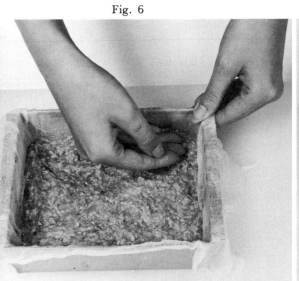

Fig. 7

Fig. 8

Fig. 9

Omelet Block (see illustration on p. 66)

    3 eggs
    stock, about ⅓ the volume of the
        eggs
    ¼ tsp salt
    ½ tsp soy sauce
    ½ tsp *mirin* (sweetened sakè) or
        sweet sherry
    ½ tsp sugar
    about 1 tsp oil

Fig. 10

1) Beat the eggs well but do not allow them to foam.

2) Combine the eggs with ⅓ their volume of stock, the soy sauce, sugar, and *mirin*. Stir well.

3) Heat a heavy frying pan (the rectangular kind made especially for this dish is best). Brush oil on the bottom and sides of the pan.

4) Pour ⅓ of the egg mixture into the pan. Tilt the pan so that the egg covers the entire bottom. Over a moderate heat, cook till set.

5) Tilt the pan and roll the thin layer of egg forward away from you to form a cylinder in the ordinary omelet-making way.

Fig. 11

6) Once again, brush oil on the bottom and sides of the pan, raising the cooked egg to allow the oil to go under it (Fig. 10). Pour another third of the egg mixture in the pan. Raise the cooked egg to allow the mixture to flow under it. Cook and roll in the same way as before (Figs. 11 and 12).

7) Repeat with the remaining third of the mixture. If prepared in the Japanese pan, the omelet will now be a rectangular solid. Turn the omelet out on a napkin, or better still, on a bamboo mat (*sudare*) made for this purpose (Figs. 13 and 14). Roll to adjust the shape into a flat rectangle (Fig. 15). Allow it to stand weighted with a plate for about ten minutes.

8) Unwrap and slice as desired. The omelet slices may be served as an appetizer, main dish, or garnish.

Fig. 12

Serves four.

Fig. 13

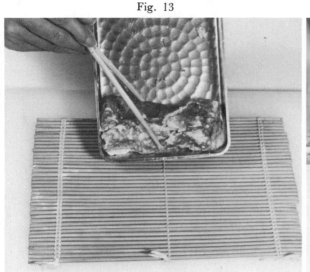

Fig. 14

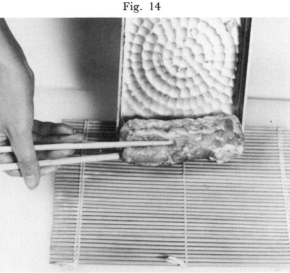

Savory Egg Custard

(see illustration on p. 66)

Fig. 15

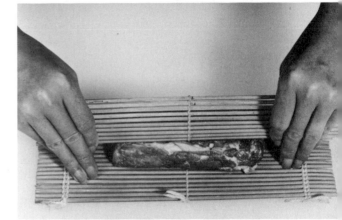

6 eggs
1½ cups stock
⅔ tsp salt
1 tsp sakè
a few circular slices of carrot
1 dried *shiitake* mushroom

1)   Soak the mushroom in warm water till softened. Remove and discard the stem and cube the cap. Cut the carrot slices into floral shapes.

2)   Beat the eggs lightly and stir in stock, salt, and sakè. Strain the mixture (Fig. 16) and add the carrots and mushroom.

3)   Line a square cake pan or baking dish about 3 in (8 cm) deep with aluminum foil. Oil the foil lightly. Pour in the egg mixture.

4)   In an oriental-style steamer, steam the custard mixture for four minutes over a high heat. Lower the heat and steam for another twenty minutes.

5)   Dip the bottom of the pan in ice water and run a sharp knife around the inside edge to release the custard or invert a plate on the pan. Remove the pan, peel away the foil, and cut the custard into serving pieces.

Serves six.

Fig. 16

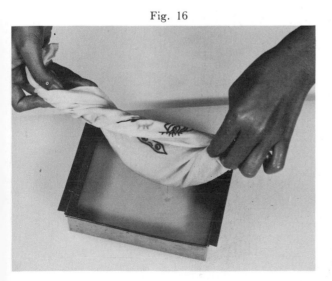

(top to bottom) Omelet block (p. 64), Japanese-style scrambled eggs (p. 68), Fancy quail eggs for garnish (p. 68), Savory egg custard (p. 65), Steamed egg and chicken layers (p. 62)

(top to bottom)   Chilled bean curd (p. 72), Scrambled bean curd (p. 72), Bean-curd burgers (p. 77), Deep-fried bean curd (p. 73)

Fig. 17

Fig. 18

Japanese-style Scrambled Eggs

(see illustration on p. 66)

> ¼ lb (100 g) cubed chicken meat
> 10 oz (280 g) chopped trefoil or
>   scallions
> 4 eggs
> 2 Tbsp stock
> 1 tsp sugar
> 1 tsp salt
> few drops soy sauce
> 2 Tbsp oil

Fig. 19

1) Lightly beat eggs; add stock, sugar, salt, soy sauce; and mix well.
2) In a skillet heat oil and sauté chicken until it changes color (Fig. 17). Add trefoil (or scallions) and stir-fry for a few seconds (Fig. 18).
3) Pour in eggs (Fig. 19) and fry in the usual manner for scrambled eggs.

Serves two.

Fancy Quail Eggs for Garnish

(see illustration on p. 66)

> 16 quail eggs
> salt

Boil the quail eggs for ten minutes, stirring frequently to ensure that the yolks will be in the middle of the hard-boiled eggs.

Peep-through Eggs: Shell nine of the quail eggs. Score them with a sharp knife lengthwise and at equal intervals all the way around (Fig. 20). Stand one of the eggs on its thick end on a piece of damp cloth. Drape the cloth over the egg and press firmly but lightly on the top (Figs. 21 and 22). Do not crush the egg. Unwrap. The yolk will be peeping through the incisions in the white.

Egg Rabbits: Heat the point of an icepick or a metal skewer and burn marks for ears and mouth on the small end of a hardboiled quail egg; with a toothpick and some red food coloring make pink eyes.

Egg Blossoms: Cut a thick slice of raw potato. Into the center of it, insert five long bamboo skewers in a circle slightly smaller than the diameters of the hardboiled quail eggs (Fig. 23). Stack six eggs, one on the

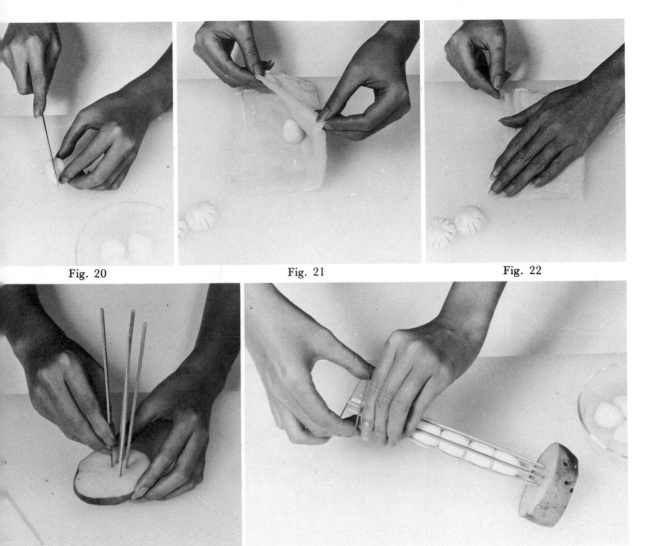

Fig. 20 | Fig. 21 | Fig. 22

Fig. 23 | Fig. 24

Fig. 25

other, among the bamboo skewers and secure the open end with a rubber band (Figs. 24 and 25). The skewers must make indentations in the egg whites. Prepare a dilute solution of red food coloring and water. Allow the stacked eggs to soak in this for from thirty minutes to an hour. Remove eggs from among the skewers and cut crosswise in half.

Serves four.

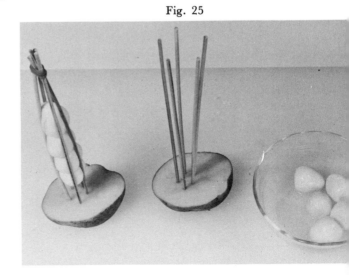

(left to right)   Oriental combination salad
(p. 88), Cucumbers and shrimp with ginger
(p. 89), Broccoli in mustard sauce (p. 90),
Marinated cauliflower (p. 88), Japanese tuna
salad (p. 89), Chrysanthemum turnips (p.
90), Celery in sesame sauce (p. 90)

Bean Curd and Beans

Chilled Bean Curd *(Hiya Yakko)*

(see illustration on p. 67)

    2 cakes bean curd
    6 Tbsp soy sauce
GARNISHES
    2 Tbsp chopped scallion
    ¼ cup shaved dried bonito *(katsuo-bushi)*

1)   Cut each bean-curd cake into four equal pieces. Rinse, drain, and chill well.
2)   Combine soy sauce and garnish in small bowls.
3)   Serve the cold bean curd in individual dishes accompanied by the soy-sauce mixture. Pieces of curd are dipped into the soy sauce before being eaten.

Serves four.

Scrambled Bean Curd

(see illustration on p. 67)

    2 cakes bean curd
    ½ cup shredded carrot
    ½ cup shredded string beans
    ½ cup shredded *shiitake* mushrooms or champignons
    2 eggs
    ¼ cup boiled green peas
    2 Tbsp sakè or dry sherry
    2 Tbsp soy sauce
    1 Tbsp sugar
    2 Tbsp stock
    oil

1)   Boil bean curd (Fig. 1). Drain and beat with an egg beater until coarsely broken.
2)   Combine shredded carrot, string beans, and mushrooms with 1 Tbsp sakè, soy sauce, sugar, and stock and cook over a moderate flame till the liquid has evaporated (Figs. 2 and 3).
3)   In a heavy pan, heat oil. Sauté the bean curd till it is well coated with oil. Add the shredded vegetables and stir fry. Add remaining seasonings.
4)   Beat the eggs lightly and add to the pan (Fig. 4). Over a medium heat mix well. Sprinkle with green peas before serving.

Serves four.

Fig. 1

Fig. 2

Fig. 3

Fig. 4

Deep-fried Bean Curd

(see illustration on p. 67)

2 cakes bean curd
4 Tbsp cornstarch or flour
oil for frying

SAUCE

1 tsp sugar
⅓ cup soy sauce
¼ cup *mirin* (sweetened sakè) or sweet sherry
½ cup stock
¼ cup shredded scallion
1 tsp grated ginger

1) Chill scallions in cold water for several minutes. Drain well.
2) Wrap the bean curd in a cloth or in paper towels, weight it, and allow it to stand for fifteen minutes. Cut each cake in half.
3) Coat each piece of bean curd in cornstarch (Fig. 5). Heat oil (180 degrees C or 350 degrees F) and deep-fry the bean curd about one minute and a half (Fig. 6). Remove and drain.
4) In a saucepan combine sugar, soy sauce, and stock and bring to a boil.
5) Arrange the bean curd on a serving plate and top with the sauce, scallions and grated ginger.

Serves four.

Fig. 5

Fig. 6

(left to right) Stuffed squash (p. 94), Sesame-sauce spinach (p. 93), Bean sprouts in sesame sauce (p. 91), String beans in sesame sauce (p. 93), Deep-fried eggplant (p. 94), Potatoes in meat sauce (p. 91)

Fig. 7 Bean curd in chicken sauce

Bean Curd in Chicken Sauce

        2 cakes bean curd
        3 cups water
        1 Tbsp crushed ginger root
        1 Tbsp soy sauce
        1 Tbsp sugar
        ½ tsp salt
    CHICKEN SAUCE
        6 oz (170 g) ground chicken meat
        3 Tbsp soy sauce
        1 Tbsp sugar
        2 Tbsp cornstarch

1) Cut each cake of bean curd in half. In a deep pot, combine water, soy sauce, sugar, salt, and ginger. Bring to a boil, add the bean curd, and simmer, taking care not to break the curd, for about five minutes (Fig. 8).
2) Combine two cups of the stock in which the bean curd was cooked with soy sauce and sugar (Fig. 9). Add the ground chicken meat (Fig. 10).
3) Reduce liquid slightly over a medium heat. Add the cornstarch (Fig. 11) and, stirring constantly, cook till thickened.
4) Remove the bean curd carefully from stock to a deep serving plate, top with the chicken sauce, and serve at once.

Serves four.

Fig. 8

Fig. 9

Fig. 10

Fig. 11

Bean-curd Burgers

(see illustration on p. 67)

 2 cakes bean curd
 7 oz (200 g) canned crab meat
 3 chopped fresh *shiitake* mushrooms
 1 medium chopped carrot
 1 egg
 oil
 1 tsp salt

SAUCE

 1 tsp mustard
 2 Tbsp soy sauce

1) Wrap bean curd in cheese cloth and allow it to stand, weighted with a board, for a while (Figs. 12 and 13).

Fig. 12

Fig. 13

(top to bottom) Variety sushi (p. 107), Sushi-stuffed fried bean curd (p. 109), Laver-rolled sushi (p. 110)

(top to bottom)   Bean-paste soup (p. 118), Hard-boiled egg and thin noodles in broth (p. 120),
Egg-ribbon soup (p. 120), Clam soup (p. 119), Soup with chicken meat balls (p. 118)

Fig. 14

Fig. 15

Fig. 16

2) Carefully pick over the crab meat to remove all membrane. Flake it.

3) Put the bean curd through a food chopper or pound it in an earthenware mortar (*suribachi*) (Fig. 14). Combine it with the egg, mushrooms, carrot, and salt (Fig. 15). Mix well. Add the crab meat. Mix again (Fig. 16).

4) Shape the mixture into patties, using about ½ cup each (Figs. 17–19).

5) In a frying pan, heat oil and fry the patties till golden brown. Serve with a mixture of mustard and soy sauce.

Serves four.

Fig. 17

Fig. 18

Fig. 19

Fig. 20   Stir-fried snow

Stir-fried Snow

3 cups soybean pulp *(okara)*
4 Tbsp oil
½ cup chopped scallion
1 cup boiled or canned shrimp
4 dried *shiitake* mushrooms
4 oz (100 g) shredded carrot
½ cup stock (include water in which
   mushrooms has been soaked)
2 Tbsp sugar
4 Tbsp soy sauce
1 Tbsp *mirin* (sweetened sakè) or
   sweet sherry

1)   Soften the mushrooms in warm water. Remove and discard the stems and shred the caps.
2)   Mix stock, sugar, soy sauce, and *mirin* with mushrooms and carrot. Simmer for fifteen minutes.
3)   Heat oil in a frying pan and stir-fry scallions and shrimp briefly. Add soybean pulp and stir-fry over low heat till fluffy.
4)   Add cooked vegetables and simmer together until liquid has evaporated and the mixture is light.

Serves four.

Fig. 21   Ingredients for stir-fried snow

Note: Okara, the pulp left after the preparation of bean curd from soybeans, is usually available from bean-curd manufacturers. Dried shrimp, soaked, drained, and coarsely chopped may be used in place of boiled or canned shrimp.

Fig. 22   Stuffed bean-curd bags

Stuffed Bean-curd Bags

    4 fried bean-curd cases *(abura-age)*
    8 pieces *kampyo* gourd 6½ in (about
      13 cm) long

FILLING
    6 oz (170 g) chopped chicken meat
    2 eggs
    1 cake bean curd
    5 dried *shiitake* mushrooms
    1 Tbsp sakè or dry sherry
    1 Tbsp sugar
    1 Tbsp soy sauce

SOUP
    2 cups stock
    3 Tbsp sakè or dry sherry
    2 Tbsp sugar
    3 Tbsp soy sauce

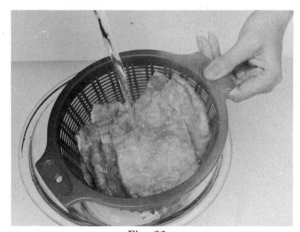

Fig. 23

1)   Make eight bean-curd bags by cutting the four pieces of *abura-age* in half. Remove some of the oil by pouring hot water over them (Fig. 23). Separate them into bag shapes.

2) Soak dried *shiitake* mushroom in warm water till softened. Remove and discard the stems and chop the caps.

3) Drain the bean curd, chop fine, and mix with two lightly beaten eggs.

4) Combine chopped chicken, mushrooms, sakè, sugar, and soy sauce and bring to a boil. Remove from heat and combine with bean-curd mixture.

5) Boil *kampyo* strips in hot water to soften them.

6) Stuff the *abura-age* bags with the chicken-meat mixture (Fig. 24). Fold the tops down and tie with *kampyo* strips (Figs. 25 and 26).

7) In a deep pot, combine the soup ingredients and boil the stuffed bags for twenty minutes over a low heat (Fig. 27).

Serves four.

Fig. 24

Fig. 25

Fig. 26

Fig. 27

Fig. 28 Boiled soybeans

Boiled Soybeans

    1 cup dry soybeans
    3 Tbsp soy sauce
    ½ cup sugar
    2 Tbsp sakè or dry sherry
    4 cups water

1) Wash the beans and soak in plenty of water overnight.
2) Drain the beans. In a deep pot, combine them with 4 cups of water. Bring to a boil. Lower the heat. Add soy sauce, sugar, and sakè. Simmer for an hour and a half, or until the beans are tender.

Serves four.

Fig. 29

Fig. 30

Quick Homemade Bean Curd

    1 cup soybeans
    15 cups water
    1 Tbsp solidifier (calcium sulfate)
       (0.5 percent the quantity of soybean milk)

1) Wash soybeans and soak in 5 cups of water overnight (Figs. 29–31). Rinse and drain.

Fig. 31

Fig. 32

2) Put beans in a blender and add an equal quantity of water. Blend at high speed for about three minutes or until a smooth purée is formed (Fig. 32).

3) Combine the purée with seven cups of water in a large pot and bring to a boil, stirring constantly to prevent sticking (Fig. 33).

4) When foam rises, turn the heat off at once.

5) Stretch cheese cloth across the mouth of a large container. Strain the hot mixture (Figs. 34–36) to separate what is called soybean milk from the pulp (*okara*), which can be reserved for use in other recipes (see p. 81).

Fig. 33

Fig. 34

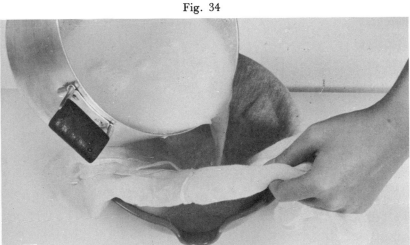

Fig. 35

Fig. 36

6) Allow the soybean milk to cool to about 70 degrees C or 136 degrees F. Dissolve the solidifier in 8 Tbsp of water. Add half of this to the soybean milk, mix lightly (Figs. 37 and 38), cover, bring to a boil (Fig. 39); lower the heat and simmer for about five minutes.

7) Add the remaining solidifier (Fig. 40). Stir well and cover. After a short while, curds should appear in clear yellow liquid. If all of the liquid does not curdle in a reasonable amount of time, wait one minute, then stir to stimulate curdling. If this still does not completely curdle the liquid, dissolve a small additional amount of solidifier in water and add it to the container.

Fig. 37

Fig. 38

Fig. 39

8) A square box with holes in the bottom lined with wet cheese cloth is a good settling container. [The curds should form a layer about 3 in (8 cm) deep.] Ladle them into the box, and cover with a wooden lid or with more cheese cloth (Figs. 41–43). Allow the bean curd to drain in the sink for about six minutes. Unwrap it and gently transfer it to a large container of fresh water until you are ready to use it (Fig. 44). It will keep for about three days in fresh water.

Fig. 40

Fig. 41

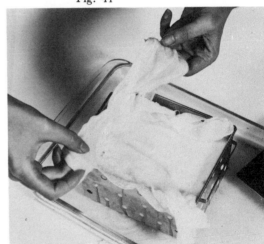

Fig. 42

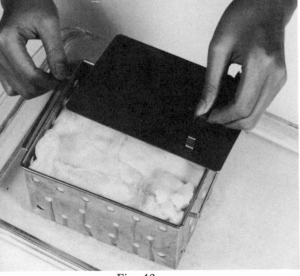

Fig. 43

Fig. 44

Vegetables

Marinated Cauliflower

(see illustration on p. 71)

1 small (10 oz or 250 g) head cauliflower
1 tsp vinegar
SEASONINGS
½ cup vinegar
2 Tbsp sugar
3 Tbsp water
1 small red chili pepper

1) Remove leaves and base of stalk from
cauliflower and separate it into florets
(Fig. 1). Boil in water containing 1 tsp
vinegar until tender. Plunge in cold water
at once. Chill.

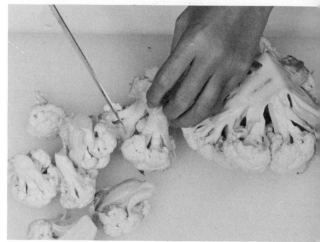

Fig. 1

2) Combine seasonings in a saucepan and
bring to a boil. Chill and pour over cold
cauliflower. Serve cold.

Serves four.

Oriental Combination Salad

(see illustration on p. 70)

½ cucumber
1 stalk celery
½ carrot
SAUCE
2 Tbsp soy sauce
2 Tbsp vinegar
½ tsp sugar
1 tsp sesame oil

Fig. 2

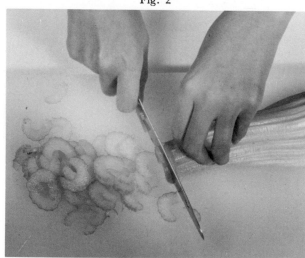

Fig. 3

1) Cut vegetables into thin strips (Figs. 2
and 3).
2) Combine sauce ingredients.
3) Arrange a heap of celery, a separate
heap of carrot, and another heap of cucumber on a serving plate. Top with the sauce
and serve cold.

Serves four.

Japanese Tuna Salad

(see illustration on p. 71)

> ½ can tuna
> 2 stalks celery
> 1 Tbsp sesame oil
> ¼ tsp salt
> 3 Tbsp vegetable oil

1) Wash and scrape celery. Slice thin crosswise.
2) Press the oil from and flake the tuna.
3) Combine tuna, celery, and seasonings. Mix well and chill before serving.

Serves two.

Cucumbers and Shrimp with Ginger (see illustration on p. 70)

> ½ cucumber
> 10 medium shrimp
> dash of salt

SEASONINGS

> 3 Tbsp vinegar
> 2 Tbsp stock
> 1 Tbsp soy sauce
> 1 tsp juice extracted from crushed fresh ginger root

Fig. 4

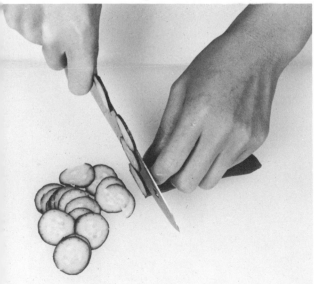

1) Slice cucumber thin (Fig. 4). Sprinkle it with salt. Allow to stand for five minutes. Squeeze well to remove as much moisture as possible.
2) Combine shrimp and cucumber slices.
3) Combine seasonings, pour over shrimp and cucumber, mix well, and chill.

Serves four.

Marinated Cucumbers with Shrimp (see illustration on back jacket)

> 2 (8 oz or 200 g) medium cucumbers
> 4 medium shrimp
> 2 oz (50 g) dried *wakame* seaweed
> julienne-cut peel from ½ lemon

MARINADE

> ⅓ cup vinegar
> 1 Tbsp sugar
> ⅓ tsp soy sauce
> ⅓ tsp salt

1) Peel and devein the shrimp. Boil in hot water for three minutes. Drain and cut in 1-in (3 cm) pieces.
2) Combine the marinade ingredients. Marinate shrimp in this mixture.
3) Soften the *wakame* seaweed in warm water. Cut off and discard tough parts. Cut the seaweed in 1-in (3 cm) pieces. The seaweed may be parboiled for increased tenderness. After soaking, the weight of the seaweed will have roughly quadrupled.
4) Slice the cucumbers thin, salt them lightly, and allow them to stand for five minutes. Squeeze them well.
5) Combine the seaweed, cucumber and shrimp in marinade. Heap on a serving plate and top with the julienne-cut lemon peel.

Serves four.

Fig. 5

Broccoli in Mustard Sauce

(see illustration on p. 70)

> 1 medium stalk broccoli
> salt

SAUCE
> 1 Tbsp mustard
> 1 Tbsp sakè or dry sherry
> 1 Tbsp vinegar
> 2 Tbsp soy sauce

1) Boil broccoli in salted water for five minutes. Plunge at once in cold water. Drain.
2) Cut into suitable pieces (Fig. 5) and chill.
3) Mix sauce ingredients.
4) Toss the sauce and the broccoli pieces together. Chill well.

Serves four.

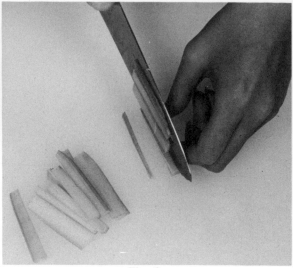

Fig. 6

Celery in Sesame Sauce

(see illustration on p. 71)

> 2 stalks celery

SAUCE
> 1 Tbsp sesame paste (or peanut butter)
> 2 tsp mustard
> 2 Tbsp mayonnaise

1) Combine sauce ingredients.
2) Cut celery in thin strips (Fig. 6).
3) Mix celery and sauce and chill well.

Serves two.

Chrysanthemum Turnips

(see illustration on p. 71)

> 5 or 6 small turnips

SEASONINGS
> 1½ Tbsp sugar
> 3 Tbsp vinegar
> ½ tsp salt
> 1 red chili pepper cut into thin rings

1) Peel the turnips.
2) A convenient way to produce a flower effect is to put each turnip between two chopsticks on a chopping board. With a

Fig. 7

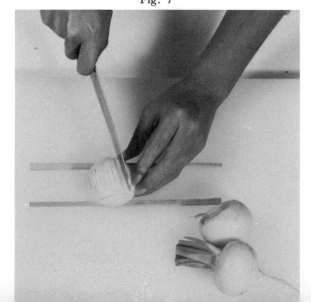

thin, sharp knife, slice thin from the top (Fig. 7). The chopsticks will prevent the knife from going all the way to the board. The turnip will therefore remain connected at the bottom. Turn the turnip and slice again at right angles with the first incisions. Continue in the same way with the other turnips.

4) Sprinkle the turnips with salt and weight them with a plate or board. Wash them and carefully squeeze out as much moisture as possible.

5) Combine the seasonings. Marinate the turnips in this mixture for half an hour.

6) Whole or halved, these flowerlike turnips make an attractive pickled garnish.

Serves two.

Potatoes in Meat Sauce

(see illustration on p. 75)

> 5 or 6 medium white potatoes
> ½ lb (220 g) ground pork
> 2 cups stock
> ½ tsp salt
> 2 Tbsp sakè or dry sherry
> 1½ Tbsp sugar
> 1 Tbsp soy sauce
> 1 Tbsp cornstarch
> ¼ cup water

1) Peel and wash potatoes. Cut into 1-in (3 cm) cubes.

2) Sauté pork in a heated frying pan until it changes color. Add potatoes and sauté quickly (Fig. 8).

3) Add stock, salt, sakè, sugar, and soy sauce (Fig. 9). Bring to a boil. Lower the heat and simmer until the potatoes are tender.

4) Dissolve cornstarch in ¼ cup water.

5) Pour cornstarch mixture into the potato-pork mixture. Cook until the sauce thickens. Remove from the heat at once and serve hot.

Serves four.

Fig. 8

Fig. 9

Bean Sprouts in Sesame Sauce

(see illustration on p. 74)

> ½ lb (220 g) bean sprouts
> ⅓ tsp salt
>
> SAUCE
>
> 1 Tbsp sesame paste or peanut butter
> 1 Tbsp sugar
> 1 Tbsp soy sauce

1) Parboil the bean sprouts for no more than twenty seconds in boiling salted water. Plunge them into cold water at once. Drain well.

2) Combine sauce ingredients and marinate the bean sprouts in the mixture. Serve cold.

Serves two.

Ginger-soy-sauce Eggplant

Fig. 10

3 (½ lb or 220 g) small eggplants
1 tsp grated fresh ginger root
1 Tbsp soy sauce

1) Wash eggplants. Broil them or grill them till the meat is tender and the skin cracked and burned (Fig. 10).
2) Plunge them into cold water and peel at once (Fig. 12). Wash well. Wipe with paper towels.
3) Serve warm and topped with soy sauce and grated ginger.

Serves two.

Fig. 11 Ginger-soy-sauce eggplant

Fig. 12

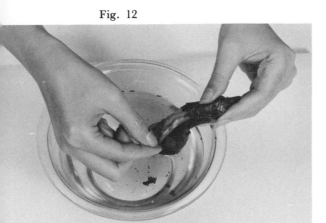

Fig. 13

Fig. 14

Sesame-sauce Spinach

(see illustration on p. 74)

½ lb (220 g) spinach

SAUCE

4 Tbsp white sesame seeds
1 Tbsp soy sauce
1 Tbsp sakè or dry sherry
½ tsp hot pepper or a few drops of
pepper sauce
1 tsp crushed garlic
1 Tbsp vinegar
1 Tbsp sugar

1) Carefully wash spinach, parboil in salted water (Fig. 13), plunge in cold water, and drain.
2) Toast sesame seeds till they begin to pop (the sesame toaster in Fig. 14 is convenient for this purpose.). Be careful since the seeds burn easily. Crush in a mortar or in a blender. Combine with other sauce ingredients.
3) Bunch the spinach, separate the roots, and cut the leaves into 2 in (5 cm) lengths. Arrange on a serving plate and top with the sauce.

Serves two.

String Beans in Sesame Sauce

(see illustration on p. 75)

½ lb (220 g) string beans

SAUCE

4 Tbsp sesame paste or peanut butter
3 Tbsp soy sauce
2 Tbsp sugar
1 Tbsp stock

1) String the beans and parboil for from five to six minutes in salted water. Plunge in cold water and drain. Cut into convenient lengths.
2) Combine sauce ingredients to make a smooth paste.
3) Add beans and mix well. Heap the beans on a serving plate and top them with the remaining sauce.

Serves two.

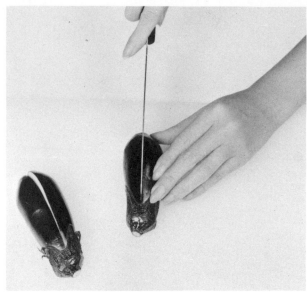

Fig. 15

Deep-fried Eggplant

(see illustration on p. 75)

        2 or 3 small eggplants
        oil for deep frying

SAUCE

        1 Tbsp oil
        2 Tbsp bean paste *(miso)*
        1 Tbsp sugar
        ½ Tbsp sakè or dry sherry
        2 Tbsp sesame seeds

1)   Make a deep lengthwise incision almost all the way through each of the eggplants (Fig. 15).
2)   In hot oil, deep fry eggplants until they are tender. Drain on paper towels.
3)   Toast the sesame seeds in a skillet until they are fragrant. Set aside.
4)   Heat 1 Tbsp oil in a heavy skillet. Add bean paste, sugar, and sakè. Stirring constantly, cook until the mixture is smooth.
5)   Spread the bean-paste mixture in the incisions in the fried eggplants. Arrange them on a serving plate and sprinkle with toasted sesame seeds.

Serves two.

Stuffed Squash (see illustration on p. 74)

        1 medium summer squash
        ½ lb (220 g) shrimp
        5 eggs
        ½ cup fresh or frozen green peas
        1 tsp salt

SAUCE

        ½ cup stock
        1 Tbsp cornstarch
        dash salt
        dash pepper

1)   Cut off top of squash about 1 in (3 cm) from the base of the stem. Scoop out and discard the seeds. Steam the squash in an oriental-style steamer or on a rack in about 2 in (5 cm) of boiling water in the bottom of a heavy pot (Fig. 16).
2)   Meanwhile, shell and devein the shrimp. Make incisions in the bodies to prevent further curling. Boil for about three minutes or until color changes.
3)   Beat eggs lightly with salt. Scramble-fry the cooked shrimp and eggs together.
4)   When the squash is tender, fill it with the scrambled egg and shrimp. Top with canned or cooked green peas.
5)   Heat stock with salt and pepper. Combine cornstarch with 2 Tbsp water. Add cornstarch mixture to the hot soup and cook until the mixture thickens. Pour this sauce on the stuffed squash.
6)   Serve by spooning out helpings of both squash and scrambled eggs.

Serves four.

Fig. 16

Sea Vegetables

Fig. 1 Mixed seaweeds salad

Mixed Seaweeds Salad

2 or 3 kinds of edible seaweeds (For instance, 1 cup each of red, green, and white *tosaka-so* (cockscomb) seaweed)

SAUCE

1 Tbsp vinegar
2 Tbsp soy sauce
1 tsp sugar
2 Tbsp sesame oil
toasted sesame seeds

1) Wash all seaweeds thoroughly, taking care to remove grit. If the seaweeds are salted, soak them till all traces of salt have been removed.

2) Mix the sauce ingredients.

3) Arrange the seaweeds on a heap of ice cubes on a serving plate. Pour the sauce into a separate bowl, sprinkle lightly with toasted sesame seeds. The seaweeds are dipped into the sauce just before being eaten.

Serves two.

Fig. 2 *Wakame* seaweed with cucumbers

Wakame **Seaweed with Cucumbers**

    1 large cucumber
    2 oz (50 g) *wakame* seaweed
    1 Tbsp minced fresh ginger root
    ⅓ tsp salt
SAUCE
    2 Tbsp vinegar
    1 tsp sugar
    ¼ tsp salt
    1 tsp soy sauce

1)   Slice the cucumber thin, sprinkle it with salt, and allow it to stand for a few minutes. Squeeze it to remove as much moisture as possible.
2)   Soften the *wakame* seaweed in warm water and cut off and discard the tough parts (Fig. 3). Cut into bite-size pieces. Drain.
3)   Combine vinegar, sugar, salt, soy sauce, and ginger. Toss the *wakame* seaweed and cucumbers in this sauce and chill.

Serves two.

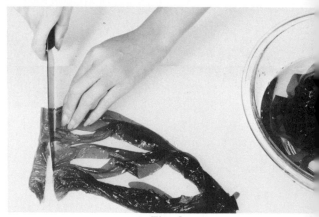

Fig. 3

Kelp Rolls

    8 pieces dried kelp (*kombu*) 4 in (10 cm) by 6 in (18 cm)
    ½ lb (220 g) thinly sliced lean pork
    8 4 in (13 cm) strips of dried *kampyo* gourd
    2 cups of water in which kelp has been soaked
    4 Tbsp soy sauce
    2 Tbsp sugar
    2 Tbsp *mirin* (sweetened sakè) or sweet sherry

Fig. 4

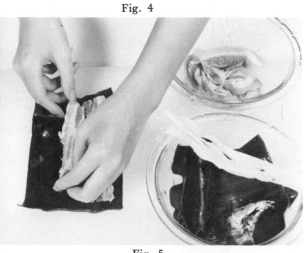

1) Wipe the kelp well and soak it in water till soft. Retain 2 cups of the water.

2) Soak the *kampyo* gourd strips in water till soft.

3) Spread a strip of kelp on a chopping board. Top with a slice of raw pork (Fig. 4). Roll and tie in the middle with a strip of *kampyo* gourd (Figs. 5 and 6).

4) Combine 2 cups of water in which kelp was soaked, soy sauce, sugar, and *mirin*. Add the kelp rolls. Bring to a boil and simmer for thirty minutes or until tender.

Serves four.

Fig. 5

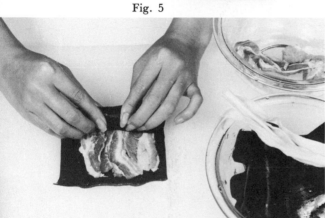

Fig. 6

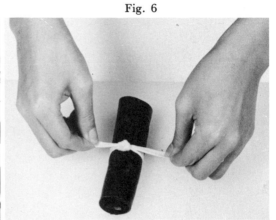

Fig. 7   Kelp Rolls

Kelp Flakes with Fried Bean Curd

⅓ cup dried kelp flakes (*hijiki*, which resemble dried tea leaves)

2 (20 oz or 50 g) fried bean curd cases (*abura-age*)

1 (90 oz or 250 g) medium carrot

3 Tbsp oil

SEASONINGS

¾ cup stock

1 Tbsp sugar

4 Tbsp soy sauce

1 Tbsp *mirin* (sweetened sakè) or sweet sherry

1) Remove some of the oil from the fried bean curd by soaking it in warm water. Drain and shred.

2) Wash kelp flakes. Soak in lukewarm water for thirty minutes. They will increase in volume to about two cups. Boil for a few minutes then drain.

3) Heat oil and sauté the fried bean curd, kelp flakes, and carrot. Add seasonings and simmer for from ten to fifteen minutes or until the moisture has evaporated. Serve either hot or cold.

Serves four.

Fig. 8   Ingredients for kelp flakes with fried bean curd

Fig. 9   Kelp flakes with fried bean curd

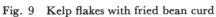

Rice

Fig. 1   Tea-and-rice soup with salmon

Tea-and-rice Soup with Salmon

2 cups cold cooked rice
2 slices salmon
trefoil or parsley for garnish
½ tsp salt
1 tsp oriental horseradish *(wasabi)*
2 Tbsp toasted sesame seeds
3½ cups stock
½ tsp salt
1 tsp soy sauce

1)   Salt the salmon on both sides and allow it to stand for about fifteen minutes. Grill and flake it coarsely.

2)   Wash the trefoil and cut it into moderately short lengths.
3)   Combine stock, salt, and soy sauce.
4)   Divide the cooked rice among four deep bowls and top with the salmon and trefoil. Sprinkle sesame seeds over the top and fill the bowls with hot stock. Garnish with a dab of horseradish.

Serves two.

Note: In ordinary homes, this dish is prepared with green tea *(cha)* instead of stock; hence it is called *chazuke.*

Fig. 2 Egg-and-chicken rice soup

Egg-and-chicken Rice Soup

2 cups cold cooked rice
4 oz (100 g) chicken meat
2 eggs
1 Tbsp chopped scallion
4 cups water
1⅓ tsp salt
1 tsp soy sauce

1) Wet-field rice prepared in the Japanese fashion has a sticky quality that is unwanted for this dish. Remove it by putting the cooked rice in a collander and running cold water over it (Fig. 3).

2) In a deep saucepan or an individual ceramic casserole combine 4 cups of water, salt, and soy sauce. Bring to a boil.

3) Cut the chicken into bite-size pieces. Add to the boiling water (Fig. 4) and, removing all scum that surfaces, cook until tender. Add the rice (Fig. 5).

4) Beat the eggs lightly and pour them in a thin stream into the boiling mixture (Fig. 6). Add the chopped scallion (Figs. 7 and 8). Cook till the egg is just barely set.

5) Serve at once in individual soup bowls.

Serves four.

Fig. 3

Fig. 4

Fig. 5

Fig. 6

Fig. 7

Fig. 8

Fig. 9   Tricolored-topped rice

Tricolored-topped Rice

     4 cups hot cooked rice

EGG TOPPING
     4 eggs
     2 Tbsp sugar
     ½ tsp salt
     2 tsp sakè or dry sherry

MEAT TOPPING
     7 oz (200 g) ground chicken meat
     2 Tbsp soy sauce
     1 Tbsp sakè or dry sherry
     1 Tbsp sugar
     ½ tsp crushed fresh ginger root

SNOW-PEAS TOPPING
     4 oz (100 g) snow peas
     ½ tsp sugar
     ½ tsp salt
     ½ cup stock

1)   Combine lightly beaten eggs, sugar, salt, and sakè. In an oiled heavy pan, over a moderate heat, stirring constantly to break the mixture into small pieces, fry till the egg is set (Fig. 10). From time to time, remove from the heat and stir vigorously to ensure a fine grain.

2)   Combine soy sauce, sakè, and sugar and bring the mixture to a boil. Add the chicken meat and cook until all the moisture has evaporated (Fig. 11).

3)   Parboil the snow peas for about three minutes in salted water. Plunge`into cold water, drain, and shred. Combine sugar, salt, and stock in a pan and cook the shredded snow peas in this mixture until the liquid has evaporated (Fig. 12).

4)   Put the hot cooked rice in serving bowls and completely cover the top of it with triangles of the three-colored toppings. No rice should be visible.

Serves two.

Fig. 10

Fig. 11

Fig. 12

1) Finely dice the chicken meat.
2) Soften the mushrooms in lukewarm water. Cut off and discard the stems. Dice the caps the same size as the chicken meat.
3) Cut the onions in half; shred.
4) Lightly beat the eggs.
5) Combine sakè, *mirin*, soy sauce, sugar, and stock. Divide the broth into four equal parts. In a small pan, boil one fourth of the chicken meat, mushrooms, and onions in one fourth of the broth till done. Pour one-quarter of the beaten egg mixture in the same pan and cook till the egg is set.
6) Divide the rice into four serving bowls. Top one serving of rice with the egg-and-chicken mixture. Sprinkle with crumbled laver and serve at once.
7) Continue with each of the other three bowls of rice and the remaining ingredients. Five Tbsp of stock may be poured over each bowl of rice for extra moisture.

Serves four.

Note: It may be more convenient to cook all the topping ingredients together at once and then put them on the four portions of cooked rice.

Hen-and-egg Rice Dish *(Oyako-domburi)*

4 cups hot cooked rice
½ lb (220 g) diced chicken meat
5 small dried *shiitake* mushrooms
1 medium onion
4 eggs
3 Tbsp sakè or dry sherry
3 Tbsp *mirin* (sweetened sakè) or sweet sherry
3 Tbsp soy sauce
1 tsp sugar
1½ cups stock
1 sheet fine-grade laver (optional)

Fig. 13　Hen-and-egg rice dish or *Oyako-donburi*

Cutlet-rice Bowl *(Katsu-don)*

    1 cup hot cooked rice
    1 boned loin pork chop fried as for
        pork cutlet (p. 34)
    1 egg
    2 stalks trefoil or shredded 2 in (5 cm)
        length of scallion
    1½ Tbsp soy sauce
    1½ Tbsp *mirin* (sweetened sakè) or
        sweet sherry
    ½ cup stock

1) Combine stock, soy sauce, and *mirin* and bring to a boil.
2) Lightly beat the egg.
3) Cut cooked cutlet into crosswise strips and put it into the pan with the stock mixture. Pour the beaten egg over and around it and sprinkle trefoil or scallion on top. Cover and cook till the egg is set.
4) Put the rice in a deep serving bowl and top with the cutlet and egg.

Serves four.

Beef-and-onion Topping on Rice *(Gyu-don)*

    1 cup hot cooked rice
    ¼ lb (100 g) thin sliced beef
    1 onion
    3 Tbsp soy sauce
    1 Tbsp sugar
    1½ Tbsp *mirin* (sweetened sakè) or
        sweet sherry
    ⅓ cup stock
    vegetable oil

1) Cut beef into narrow strips.
2) Cut onion into similar strips.
3) Heat vegetable oil in a skillet. Sauté the onion and beef till tender.
4) Combine soy sauce, sugar, *mirin*, and broth. Pour into the skillet and bring to a boil.
5) Put the hot rice in a deep individual serving bowl and top with the onion and beef. Pour the pan juices over the top and serve at once.

Serves one.

Fig. 14 Cutlet-rice bowl or *Katsu-don*

Fig. 15 Beef-and-onion topping on rice, or *Gyu-don*

Fig. 16   Tempura on rice or *Ten-don*

Tempura on Rice *(Ten-don)*

4 cups hot cooked rice
4 prawns and 4 slices onion fried as for
    tempura (see p. 51); you may use
    any other kind of tempura for this
    dish.
shredded scallion
½ cup stock
9 Tbsp soy sauce
2 Tbsp saké or dry sherry

1)   Combine stock, soy sauce, and sakè.
Bring to a boil and remove from heat.
2)   Put cooked rice in a deep individual
serving bowl. Top with tempura and shredded scallions. Pour on the hot sauce and serve
at once.

Serves four.

Variety Rice (see illustration on front jacket)

3 cups raw rice
¼ lb (100 g) *shiitake* mushrooms

½ medium carrot
½ lb (220 g) chicken meat
1 Tbsp *mirin* (sweetened sakè) or
    sweet sherry
½ tsp salt
3 cups stock

1)   Wash rice thoroughly and allow it to
drain in a colander for one hour before
cooking time.
2)   Cube chicken meat. Shred carrot and
half of the mushrooms.
3)   Combine all ingredients except the
carrot and mushrooms.
4)   Bring to a boil and simmer for five minutes covered.
5)   Add carrots and mushrooms and simmer for ten minutes more. Remove from the
heat but do not remove the lid from the
kettle for another ten minutes. The added
steaming makes the rice fluffy.

Serves four.

Rice for Sushi

2 cups raw rice
2¼ cups water
4 Tbsp vinegar
1½ Tbsp sugar
1 tsp salt

1)   Wash rice thoroughly, changing water until it runs perfectly clear.
2)   Drain and pour in exactly 2¼ cups fresh water. Bring to a boil over high heat. Lower the heat and simmer for 20 minutes. Allow the rice to steam covered until fluffy, for another fifteen minutes after being removed from the heat.
3)   Combine vinegar, sugar, and salt. Sprinkle this mixture evenly over the rice. Mix

Fig. 17

thoroughly with a wooden spatula (Fig. 17) and fan the rice all the while to produce a gloss.

Serves four.

Variety Sushi *(Chirashi-zushi)*
(see illustration on p. 78)

4 cups rice cooked for sushi
3 dried *shiitake* mushrooms
½ medium carrot
5 or 10 string beans shredded
1 sheet laver
1½ Tbsp soy sauce
1 Tbsp sugar
1 Tbsp sakè or dry sherry
½ cup stock
SHREDDED EGGS
2 eggs
⅓ tsp salt
1 Tbsp sugar

1)   Soak *shiitake* mushrooms in lukewarm water till tender. Remove and discard stems and shred caps.
2)   Scrape and shred carrot.
3)   In a saucepan combine stock, soy sauce, sugar, mushrooms, carrots, and string beans (Fig. 18).
4)   Lightly beat eggs with salt and sugar. Grease a skillet lightly (Fig. 19). Pour in part

Fig. 18

Fig. 19

Fig. 20

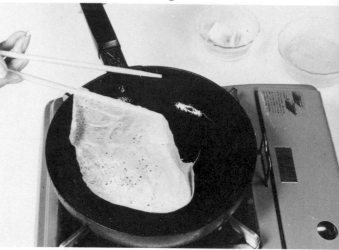

Fig. 21

Fig. 22

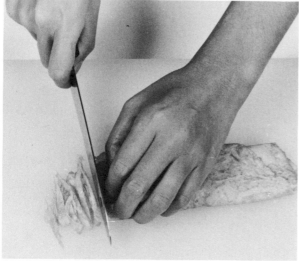

of the egg mixture and tip the pan to coat the bottom completely (Fig. 20). Cook till set. Gently lift from the pan on chopsticks, lay flat on a chopping board, and cut into thin strips (Figs. 21 and 22). Fry and shred the remaining egg in the same manner.

5)   Shred the laver (Fig. 23).

6)   Mix half of the carrot, mushrooms, string beans, and shredded eggs with the sushi rice. Heap on a serving plate and top with the remaining ingredients and the shredded laver (Fig. 24).

Serves four.

Note: Such other ingredients as crab, fish, or lotus root may be added.

Fig. 23

Fig. 24

Sushi-stuffed Fried Bean Curd

(*Inari-zushi*) (see illustration on p. 78)

> 3 cups rice cooked for sushi (p. 107)
> 5 fried-bean-curd cases *(abura-age)*
> ¾ cup stock
> 3 Tbsp sugar
> 4 Tbsp soy sauce
> 1 Tbsp sakè or dry sherry
> ⅓ cup toasted sesame seeds

1)   Put the fried-bean-curd cases in a colander and pour boiling water over them to remove some of the oil.

Fig. 25

Fig. 26

2)   In a saucepan, combine stock, sugar, soy sauce, and sakè and bring to a boil. Add the fried-bean-curd cases and simmer over a moderate heat until the liquid is reduced to one-third its original volume (Fig. 25). Cool in the sauce.

3)   Cut each of the cases to produce two small envelopes.

4)   Mix toasted sesame seeds with the sushi rice while it is still warm. Stuff the bean-curd envelopes with just enough rice to make them temptingly full (Figs. 26–28). Do not tear the fried-bean-curd cases.

Serves four.

Fig. 27

Fig. 28

Laver-rolled Sushi (*Nori-maki*)

(see illustration on p. 78)

> 3 cups rice cooked for sushi (p. 107)
> 3 sheets laver
>
> FILLING
>
> 1 oz (30 g) ham
> 1 cucumber
> 1 oz (30 g) fried egg (p. 64)
> whatever other ingredients you like

1) Cut cucumbers, ham, and fried egg in longish julienne strips.

2) Over an open flame, lightly toast a sheet of laver (Fig. 29). Spread it on a bamboo sushi-rolling mat. Leaving about ½ in (1.5· cm) at the edge closest to you, on top of the front two-thirds of the laver, make an even layer of sushi rice (Figs. 30 and 31). Along the middle, where the filling will be placed, thin the rice somewhat.

3) Place a strip of the ingredients lengthwise down the middle of the layer of sushi rice. Holding the front edge of the rolling mat between thumbs and index fingers, lift and roll till the front edge reaches the rear edge and the rice and other ingredients are neatly rolled in the sheet of laver (Figs. 32–34). Press lightly from above. (Figs. 35 and 36). Repeat with the remaining ingredients.

4) Wipe a sharp knife with a damp cloth. Place the rolls on a chopping board. Halve each one; then halve the halves (Fig. 37).

Serves four.

Note: The filling may be varied to suit individual tastes.

Fig. 29

Fig. 32

Fig. 35

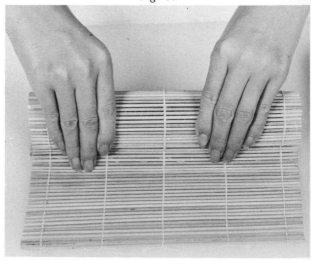

Fig. 30

Fig. 31

Fig. 33

Fig. 34

Fig. 36

Fig. 37

Rice and Green Peas

1 ½ cups raw rice
1 ½ cups stock
½ cup fresh or frozen green peas
1 tsp salt
1 Tbsp *mirin* (sweetened sakè) or
    sweet sherry

1)   About one hour before cooking time, thoroughly wash the rice until the wash water runs perfectly clear. Drain and allow to stand in a colander.
2)   Combine rice, stock, salt, and *mirin* in a heavy pot. Cover and bring to a boil over a high heat. Reduce the heat and steam for twenty minutes or until all water has been absorbed. Remove the pot from the heat and allow to stand covered for ten minutes more to make the rice fluffy.
3)   While the rice is cooking, boil the green peas till tender. Since color is important, do not overcook. Drain and reserve.
4)   Heap the rice in serving bowls and top with cooked green peas.

Serves four.

Fig. 38   Rice and green peas

Noodles

Fig. 1   Wide noodles *(udon)* in broth

Wide Noodles *(Udon)* in Broth

10 oz (280 g) *udon* noodles
1 dried *shiitake* mushroom
1 shelled, deveined shrimp
1 oz (30 g) spinach
1 egg
2 oz (50 g) cubed chicken meat

BROTH

1½ cups stock
2 Tbsp soy sauce
1 Tbsp *mirin* (sweetened sakè) or sweet
  sherry
1 tsp sugar

1)   If fresh noodles are used, pour hot water over them (Fig. 2) to separate them from each other. Dried noodles must be boiled for twenty minutes or until tender and then rinsed in cold water.

2)   Combine stock, soy sauce, and cubed chicken meat in a pot and bring to a boil (Fig. 3).

3)   Soften *shiitake* mushroom by soaking in lukewarm water. Remove and discard the stem.

4)   Clean and boil spinach. Squeeze it to remove as much moisture as possible and

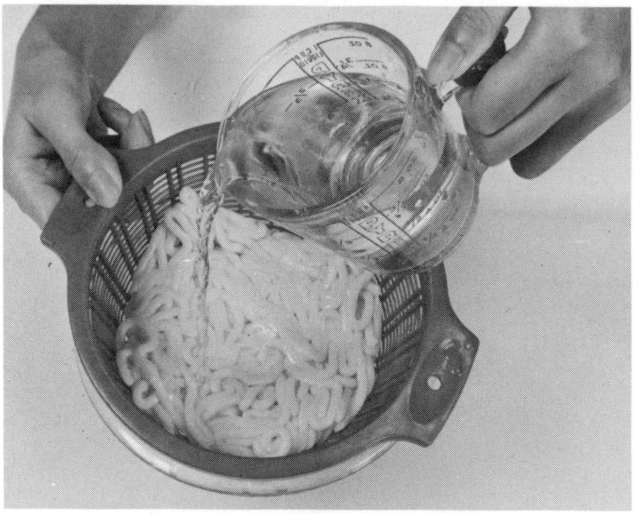

Fig. 2

Fig. 3

Fig. 4

Fig. 5

Fig. 6

Fig. 7

form it into a rough cylinder shape. Cut it into 2 in (5 cm) lengths.

5) Add *shiitake* mushroom and shrimp to the broth and simmer briefly (Fig. 4). Add noodles and simmer for from three to four minutes over a heat ranging from moderate to low (Fig. 5). Put the cut spinach on the noodles and drop a raw egg on top (Figs. 6 and 7). Simmer only until the egg is poached. Serve at once in a deep individual bowl.

Serves one.

Note: This dish is sometimes served in the kind of individual ceramic casserole (*nabe*) shown in the photographs. In such a case it is called *nabeyaki udon*.

Cold Buckwheat Noodles

1 packet buckwheat noodles *(soba)*
1 sheet dried laver
2 Tbsp chopped scallion
1 Tbsp Japanese horseradish *(wasabi)*
DIPPING SAUCE
½ cup stock
6 Tbsp soy sauce
3 Tbsp sakè or dry sherry

1) Cook the buckwheat noodles in three pints of boiling water about seven minutes or till tender (Figs. 8–10). Drain. Cool in running water. Drain again and divide into equal serving portions. Traditionally these noodles are served in bamboo baskets.

2) Shred the laver and reserve.

3) Prepare dipping sauce ahead of time to allow it to chill. Combine stock, soy sauce, and sakè in a saucepan and bring to a boil. Cool.

4) Put small portions of horseradish and chopped scallion into individual dipping bowls about the size of fairly large coffee cups. Fill the bowls about two-thirds full with chilled dipping sauce. Top the servings of noodles with chopped laver and serve. Guests take small portions of the noodles in chopsticks and dip them into the sauce before eating them.

Serves four.

Fig. 8

Fig. 9

Fig. 10

Fig. 11 Cold buckwheat noodles

Soups

Fig. 1

Fig. 2

Fig. 3

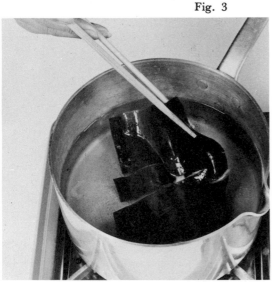

Fig. 4

Basic Stock

> 5 cups water
> 1 piece (1½ in or 4 cm) dried kelp
>   (dashi kombu)
> 1 Tbsp shaved, dried bonito* (katsuo
>   bushi)

1) Wipe the kelp lightly with a damp cloth without removing the white powdery coating (this powder greatly enhances the flavor of the stock) and stripe (Figs. 1 and 2).

2) Put kelp in water in a deep pot, bring to a boil, and remove the kelp at once (Fig. 3). If left in the boiling water it gives the stock and unpleasantly strong flavor.

3) Reduce heat to medium and add shaved bonito (Fig. 4). Turn off the heat immediately before the boiling point is reached.

*The dried bonito required for this basic stock comes either in solid bulk form, for which a special shaver is needed, or as packaged shavings.

4) Allow the flakes of dried bonito to settle to the bottom. Strain the stock into a bowl (Fig. 5). This first stock is best. A second one, made by reboiling the same kelp and bonito flakes in fresh water, is inferior to the first and should be used only in soups and dishes that are strongly flavored with such other ingredients as bean paste.

Note: A more zesty stock may be prepared from small dried fish called *niboshi*. Break them coarsely, discarding the heads, and simmer in hot water until a suitably flavored broth is produced. Sometimes a combination of kelp and *niboshi* is used. A few brands of granulated bases for Japanese stocks are marketed. They are convenient but should not be thought of as a true replacement for stock prepared the traditional way.

Fig. 5

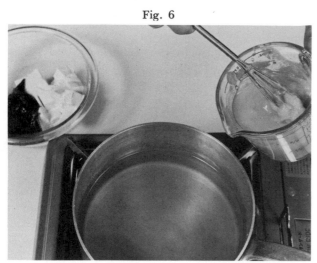

Fig. 6

Fig. 7

Bean-paste Soup *(Misoshiru)*
(see illustration on p. 79)

> 3½ cups stock
> 2 oz (50 g) bean paste
> 1 cake bean curd
> ½ oz (15 g) *wakame* seaweed

1) Cube the bean curd.
2) Soak the *wakame* seaweed in water to soften it. Cut off and discard tough parts and cut the seaweed into 1 in (3 cm) lengths.
3) In a pot slowly bring the stock to a boil. Add the bean paste and stir until it has dissolved (Fig. 6).
4) Add bean curd and *wakame* seaweed. Bring to a boil again and remove from the heat at once. The soup is traditionally served in small, lidded, lacquered bowls.

Serves four.

Soup with Chicken Meat Balls
(see illustration on p. 79)

> ½ lb (220 g) ground chicken
> 1 tsp juice extracted from crushed
>   fresh ginger root
> 1 Tbsp cornstarch
> ½ egg
> ½ tsp salt
> 4 oz (100 g) string beans

SOUP

> 3½ cups stock
> ⅔ tsp salt
> 1 tsp soy sauce

1) String the beans.
2) Combine and thoroughly mix ginger, chicken meat, cornstarch, egg, and salt.
3) Heat stock in a saucepan. Using a teaspoon, form meat balls. Drop them one by one into the hot stock (Fig. 7). Cook for about ten minutes, removing any scum that surfaces. Add salt and soy sauce. Remove from heat and add string beans. Serve hot.

Serves four.

Fig. 8

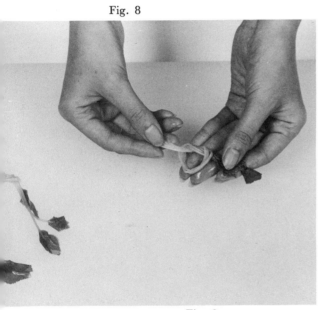

Fig. 9

Clam Soup (see illustration on p. 79)

4 clams
few stalks trefoil or spinach leaves
5-in (13 cm) piece of kelp *(dashi kombu)*
4 cups water
¾ tsp salt
1 Tbsp soy sauce

1) Soak the clams in salted water for an hour or overnight to cause them to emit grit and sand.
2) Parboil the trefoil or spinach for a few minutes, wash in cold water, and squeeze well. If you are using trefoil, tie each stalk into an attractive not (Fig. 8). Put one knot in each serving bowl. If spinach is being used, squeeze it well and cut it into convenient lengths. Put a small amount in each serving bowl.
3) Place the clams and kelp in a pot with four cups of water (Fig. 9). Bring to a boil and remove the kelp at once. Discard it. Cooking kelp too long gives stock an unpleasant taste.
4) What the clams have opened, add salt and soy sauce to taste (Fig. 10). Divide clams and broth among the serving bowls.

Serves four.

Fig. 10

Fig. 11

Egg-ribbon Soup (see illustration on p. 79)

1 egg
3 cups and 3 Tbsp stock
1 tsp soy sauce
⅔ tsp salt
1 Tbsp cornstarch
½ tsp juice extracted from crushed
  fresh ginger root

1) Beat the egg with 1 Tbsp stock.
2) Mix cornstarch with 2 Tbsp stock.
3) Bring 3 cups of stock to a boil. Add salt and soy sauce. Thicken with cornstarch mixture (Fig. 12).
4) Stirring constantly to set up a whirlpool, pour the egg mixture into the soup in a slow stream (Fig. 13). Cook only until the egg has set slightly. Serve at once.

Serves four.

Hard-boiled Egg and Thin Noodles
in Broth (see illustration on p. 79)

3½ cups stock
2 shelled, halved, hard-boiled eggs
⅔ tsp salt
1 tsp soy sauce
small amount of edible chrysanthemum leaves (*shungiku*) or spinach
1 oz (30 g) packet of thin white
  noodles (*somen*)

1) Cook *somen* noodles in plenty of boiling water for about seven minutes or until they are tender (Fig. 11). Plunge in cold running water till they are cool. Drain and reserve.
2) Parboil chrysanthemum leaves or spinach. Plunge at once in cold running water. Press into a cylindrical bunch and cut into convenient lengths.
3) Combine stock, salt, and soy sauce. Bring to a boil. Add the noodles. Divide among serving bowls and top with halved hard-boiled eggs and the green vegetable.

Serves four.

Fig. 12

Fig. 13

Fig. 14   Satsuma pork stew

Satsuma Pork Stew

  1 lb (450 g) cubed pork
  1 lb (450 g) pork bones
  4 or 5 peeled turnips or several thick
    sections of Japanese *daikon* radish
  2 sweet potatoes
  1 carrot
  2 Tbsp oil
  3 Tbsp chopped scallion
  7 Tbsp bean paste (*miso*) diluted with
    1 cup water

1)   Make a stock by boiling the pork bones
in twelve cups water for thirty minutes.
Remove scum that surfaces. Strain the stock
into a bowl and discard the bones.
2)   Peel turnips and sweet potatoes and
cut both into thick slices. Scrape carrot and
cut into thick slices.

3)   Heat 2 Tbsp oil in the bottom of a
large, heavy pot. First sauté the pork till
it changes color (Fig. 15). Then add all the
vegetables and stir till they are coated with

Fig. 15

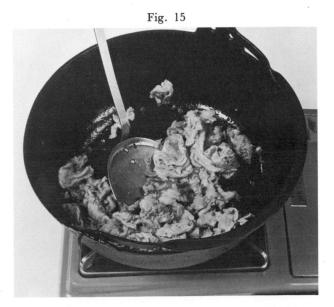

Fig. 16

oil (Figs. 16 and 17). Add six cups of stock (Fig. 18). Stir in the diluted bean paste (Fig. 19). Cover and simmer for thirty minutes or until all the ingredients are tender. Skim off scum as it forms (Fig. 20). 4) Sprinkle with chopped scallions before serving.

Serves six.

Note: Chicken may be used in place of pork.

Fig. 17

Fig. 18

Fig. 19

Fig. 20

Pickles

Fig. 1   Turnip pickles with lemon

Fig. 2

Turnip Pickles with Lemon

 3 small turnips
 ½ tsp salt
 ½ lemon
 1 Tbsp vinegar

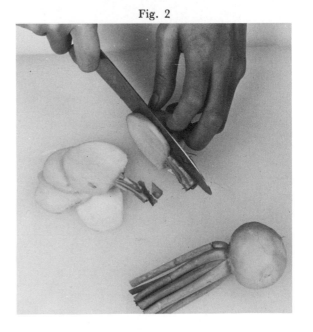

1)   Wash the turnips thoroughly. Leaving about 1 in (3 cm) of the stem intact, remove and discard the leaves. Slice thin lengthwise (Fig. 2). Sprinkle with salt and let stand for five minutes.

2)   Put the turnips in a covered container with half a lemon cut into wedges.

3)   Allow to stand for twelve hours.

Fig. 3 Pickled Chinese cabbage

Pickled Chinese Cabbage

    1 head Chinese cabbage
    1 carrot
    2 dried red chili peppers
    1 Tbsp salt

1) Make a cross-shaped incision on the base of the head of cabbage. Tear the head into four equal sections starting from this incision (Fig. 4).
2) After discarding the outer leaves, wash the cabbage.
3) Sprinkle a layer of salt on the bottom of a container (Fig. 5). Put one section of cabbage in the bottom on the salt (Fig. 6). Sprinkle the top of it with salt, rubbing some salt among the leaves.
4) Scrape and slice the carrot thin. Slice the chili peppers into thin rings.
5) Sprinkle carrot and pepper among the cabbage leaves (Fig. 7). Continue adding cabbage, salt, carrot, and pepper till all of the ingredients have been used (Fig. 8).
6) Put a heavy weight on the cabbage and allow it to stand for a few hours (Figs. 9 and 10) or overnight. Cut into bite-size pieces before serving.

Fig. 4

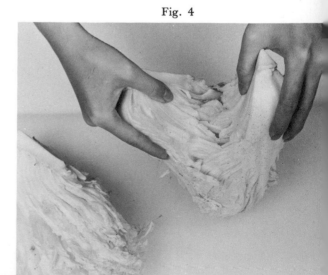

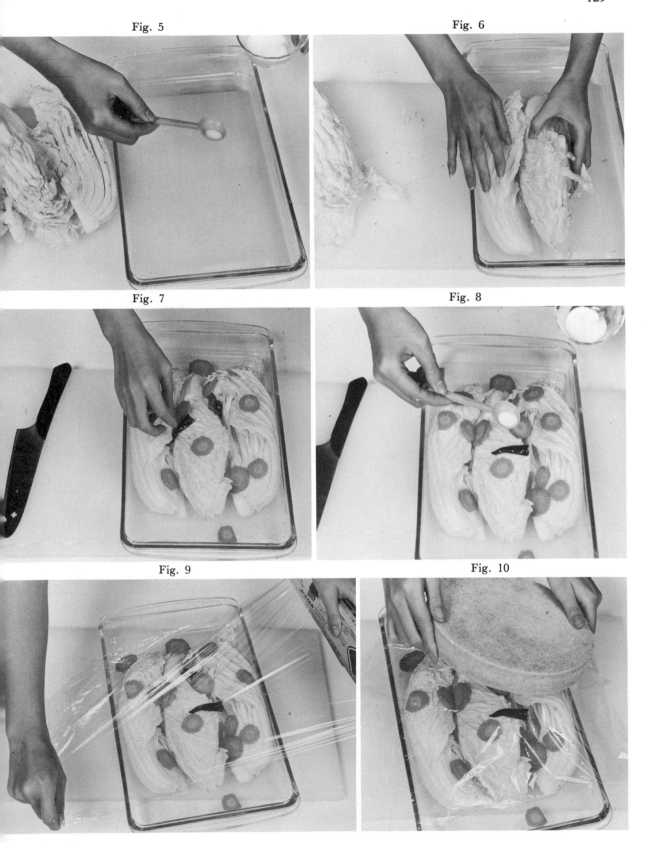

Fig. 5

Fig. 6

Fig. 7

Fig. 8

Fig. 9

Fig. 10

Fig. 11　Eggplant mustard pickles

Eggplant Mustard Pickles

　　¾ lb (300 g) eggplants
　　1 tsp salt
　　1½ Tbsp Chinese powdered mustard
　　2 Tbsp soy sauce
　　1 tsp sugar
　　1 Tbsp sakè or dry sherry

1)　Cut off and discard the eggplant stems. Cut the eggplants into bite-size pieces (Fig. 12).

2)　Soak the pieces in water for ten minutes. Drain.

3)　Sprinkle salt on the eggplants and allow them to stand weighted for two or three hours (Figs. 13–15). The photograph shows a modern plastic pickle press, but an old-fashioned board and stone or another bowl will serve as well.

4)　Meanwhile, make a paste of the mus-

tard powder and some water. Cover and allow to stand for a while to increase its piquancy.

5)　At the end of this time, combine the mustard with soy sauce, sugar, and sakè.

6)　Thoroughly squeeze the eggplants and coat well with the mustard sauce.

Fig. 12

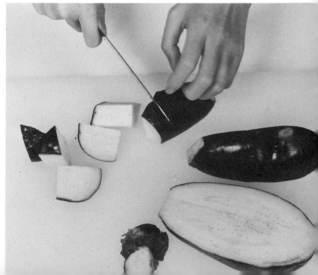

Fig. 13

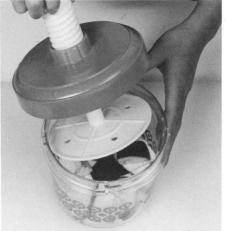

Fig. 14

Fig. 15

Celery and Carrot Pickles

1 stalk celery
1 carrot
1 Tbsp sesame oil
1 Tbsp sakè or dry sherry
2 tsp soy sauce
1 tsp sugar
1 tsp salt

Fig. 16   Celery and carrot pickles

1) Scrape and slice the celery (Fig. 17).

2) Scrape the carrot. Score it vertically all around with a fork then slice it thin (Figs. 18 and 19).

3) Combine salt, sugar, sesame oil, sakè, and soy sauce in a bowl. Add the celery and carrot. Mix well and allow to stand weighted for two hours (Figs. 20 and 21).

Fig. 17

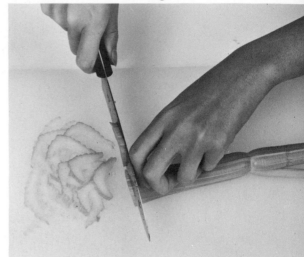

Fig. 18

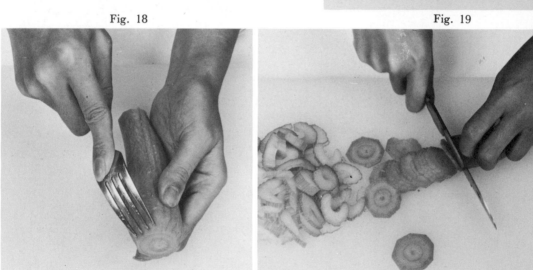

Fig. 19

Fig. 20

Fig. 21

Fig. 22 Pineapple and cucumber pickles

Pineapple and Cucumber Pickles

> ½ medium can sliced pineapple or
>   peeled, cored fresh pineapple
> 1 cucumber
> 2 Tbsp sugar
> 4 Tbsp vinegar
> 1 tsp salt

1) Peel cucumber and cut it into bite-size chunks (Fig. 23). Sprinkle with ½ tsp salt and allow to stand for 10 minutes.
2) Cut the pineapple into chunks the same size as the cucumber pieces.
3) Combine the remaining ½ tsp salt with sugar and vinegar.
4) Drain the cucumber chunks, press the moisture from them, and combine them with the pineapple pieces. Cover with the sugar-and-vinegar mixture and allow to stand for about twelve hours.

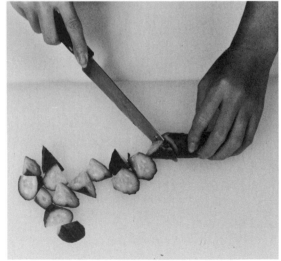

Fig. 23

Pickled Cucumbers with Sesame Seed

3 cucumbers
½ Tbsp salt
½ tsp salt
2 tsp toasted sesame seeds
1 Tbsp sakè or dry sherry
1 Tbsp sugar
2 Tbsp vinegar

1) Crush the sesame seeds in a mortar or a blender.

2) Wash the cucumbers and cut them in spirals in the following way. First cut them crosswise in half. Insert a wooden chopstick lengthwise through the whole section to make a hole. Rolling the chopstick slice the cucumber into spirals then remove the chopstick (Fig. 24).

3) Salt the cucumber spirals and allow them to stand well weighted for two or

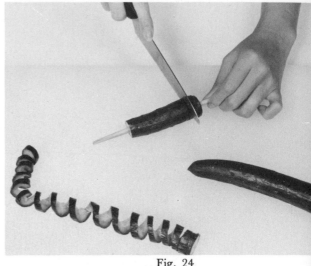

Fig. 24

three hours.

4) Combine ½ tsp salt, sesame seeds, sakè, sugar and vinegar. Just before serving, combine the salted cucumbers with this sauce.

Fig. 25 Pickled cucumbers with sesame seed

Desserts

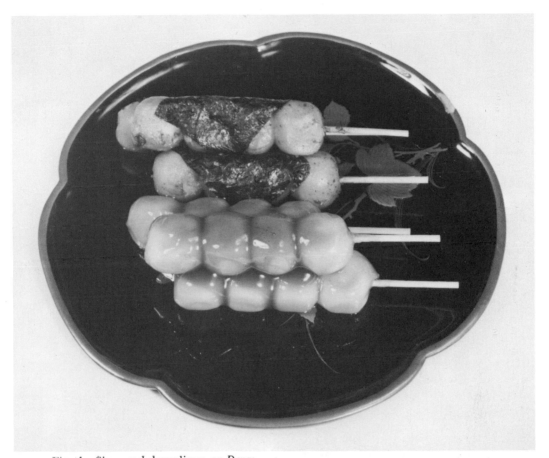

Fig. 1   Skewered dumplings, or *Dango*

Fig. 2

Skewered Dumplings (*Dango*)

    2 cups rice flour
    1½ cups hot water
    1 sheet toasted laver
    bamboo skewers

SAUCE

    3 Tbsp soy sauce
    5 Tbsp water
    2 Tbsp sugar
    1½ tsp cornstarch

1)   Combine hot water and rice flour in a bowl and mix quickly till the dough has about the resilience of your earlobe (Figs. 2–4).

Fig. 3

Fig. 4

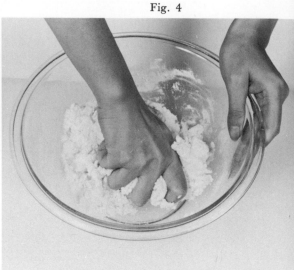

Fig. 7

2)   Form the dough into a long rod shape. Cut this in half then quarter the halves to give eight small equal pieces (Figs. 5 and 6).
3)   Bring water to a full boil in the bottom of a steamer.
4)   Shape each of the pieces of dough into a small ball (Fig. 7). Steam them in the top of the steamer for from thirteen to fifteen minutes.
5)   In a saucepan combine soy sauce, water, and sugar. Bring to a boil. Dissolve cornstarch in a small amount of water. Add this to the sauce. Cook till it is thick and clear (Fig. 8).
6)   Skewer four of the dumplings on each bamboo skewer. Over an open, moderate flame on a wire grill toast them till they are lightly browned (Fig. 9).
7)   Coat the dumplings with the sauce or top each skewer with a strip of toasted laver (Figs. 10–12).

Serves six.

Fig. 10

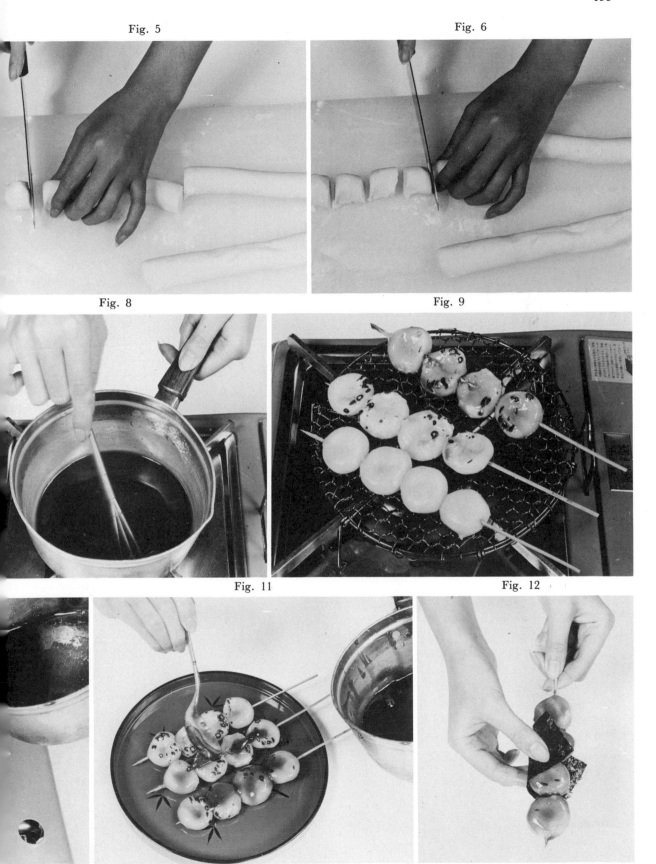

Fig. 5

Fig. 6

Fig. 8

Fig. 9

Fig. 11

Fig. 12

Fig. 13 Steamed ginger cake

Fig. 14

Fig. 15

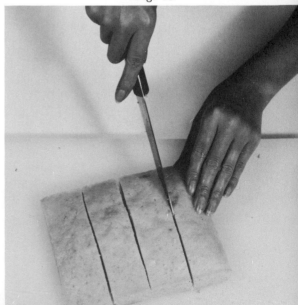

Steamed Ginger Cake

    1 cup cake flour
    1 tsp baking powder
    4 oz (100 g) brown (or white) sugar
    2 eggs
    ¼ cup water
    1 Tbsp grated ginger

1) Sift flour and baking powder together. Combine with sugar and grated ginger.
2) Lightly beat egg and combine with the flour mixture, adding water as needed to form a soft dough.
3) Put the dough in a mold.
4) Bring water to a boil in the bottom of a steamer.
5) Put the mold in the steamer, cover, and steam for twenty minutes.
6) Remove from mold and cut into serving pieces (Figs. 14 and 15).

Serves four.

Sweet-potato Balls with Chestnuts and Walnuts (Kinton)

1 lb (450 g) sweet potatoes
¾ cup sugar
¼ tsp salt
½ lb (220 g) can sweetened chestnut halves
6 shelled English walnuts
½ cup syrup from canned chestnuts
1 Tbsp cornstarch
1 Tbsp water

1) Wash, peel, and slice sweet potatoes. Boil for twenty minutes or until soft. Drain.
2) Mash the sweet potatoes with sugar and salt to produce a thick purée.
3) Force the purée through a sieve and form it into tablespoon-size balls.
4) Boil walnuts in briefly to remove the thin inner skin. Deep fry them till golden brown.
6) On a wet cloth, place one of the chestnut halves and one of the fried walnuts. Top with a ball of sweet-potato purée. Wrap the wet cloth around the mound and shape it into a ball, allowing the chestnut and walnut to remain visible (Figs. 16 and 17). Continue with the remaining ingredients.
7) In a saucepan bring the syrup from the chestnuts to a boil. Thicken with 1 Tbsp of cornstarch dissolved in 1 Tbsp of water. Pour the syrup over the sweet-potato balls (Fig. 18).

Serves four to six.

Fig. 16

Fig. 17

Fig. 18

136

Fig. 19 Sweet-potato balls with chestnuts and walnuts, or *Kinton*

Ingredient Preparations

Rounds

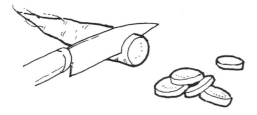

Small rounds

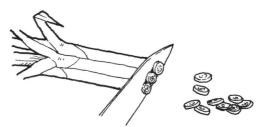

Slanting slices

Coarse cutting

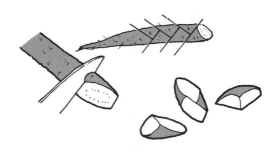

Wide rectangular slices

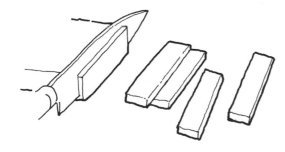

Narrow rectangular slices

Fine dice

Dice

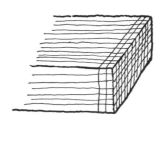

Mince

Julienne

Coarse julienne

Fine julienne

Pine-cone slicing

Chrysanthemum cut (turnips)

Cucumber fans

Notched slices

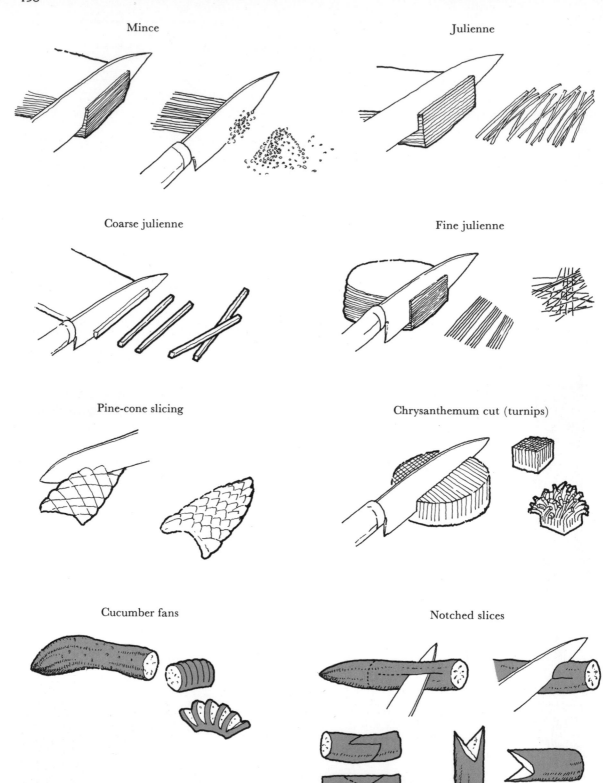

——— Incision on close side

- - - - - - Incision on far side

Utensils

(left to right) *Sashimi* knife; heavy-duty butcher knife, and general-use kitchen knife.

Long chopsticks used in food preparation.

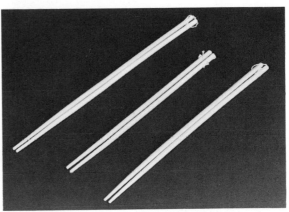

Measuring cup and spoons.

Perforated ladle.

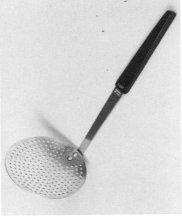

Strainer.

Rice-serving spatulas. (*Shamoji*)

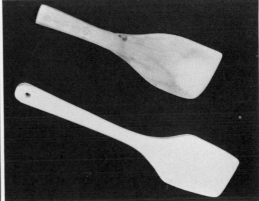

Bamboo mats for rolling *sushi* and other foods. (*Sudare*)

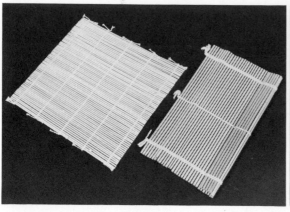

(left to right) Traditional bamboo colander and plastic colander.

Shallow pan for cooking the egg and chicken mixture used on hen-and-egg rice dish. (*Oyako-donburi Nabe*)

Rectangular pan for fried-egg block. (*Tamagoyaki Ki*)

Wire grill for use over an open flame.

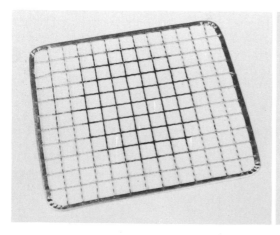

Grill with an asbestos lower plate for fish, egglant, and so on.

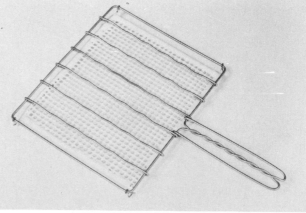

Grooved mortar and wooden pestle for crushing seeds, mashing fish, and other similar uses. (*Suribachi*)

Grater for dried bonito (*katsuo-bushi*).

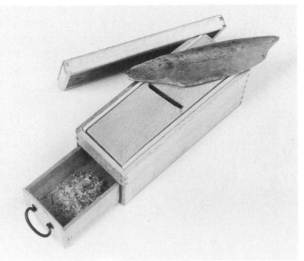

Wooden tub for preparing *sushi*.

Wire toaster for sesame seeds.

Bamboo steamer.

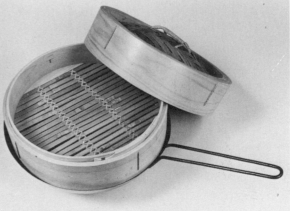

Mold with a bottom that lifts out easily; convenient for preparing egg custards, cakes, and bean curd.

Cooking brushes.

Oil storage container fitted with a strainer.

Rotary egg beater.

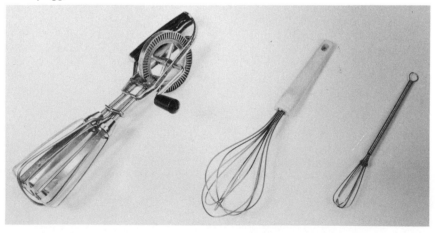

Index